Con

Acknowledegments

All translations are by the compiler except where
otherwise indicated. I would like to thank
Dario Fo, Franca Rame, Piero Sciotto,
Walter Valeri, Michael Imison and Ed Emery for
information and assistance in preparing this
Writer-File.

Tony Mitchell

The theatre is, by its nature, an ephemeral art: yet it is a daunting task to track down the newspaper reviews, or contemporary statements from the writer or his director, which are often all that remain to help us recreate some sense of what a particular production was like. This series is therefore intended to make readily available a selection of the comments that the critics made about the plays of leading modern dramatists at the time of their production — and to trace, too, the course of each writer's own views about his work and his world.

In addition to combining a uniquely convenient source of such elusive *documentation*, the 'Writer-Files' series also assembles the *information* necessary for readers to pursue further their interest in a particular writer or work. Variations in quantity between one writer's output and another, differences in temperament which make some readier than others to talk about their work, and the variety of critical response, all mean that the presentation and balance of material shifts between one volume and another: but we have tried to arrive at a format for the series which will nevertheless enable users of one volume readily to find their way around any other.

Section 1, 'A Brief Chronology', provides a quick conspective overview of each playwright's life and career. *Section 2* deals with the plays themselves, arranged chronologically in the order of their composition: information on first performances, major revivals, and publication is followed by a brief synopsis (for quick reference set in slightly larger, italic type), then by a representative selection of the critical response, and of the dramatist's own comments on the play and its theme.

Section 3 offers concise guidance to each writer's work in non-dramatic forms, while *Section 4*, 'The Writer on His Work', brings together comments from the playwright himself on more general matters of construction, opinion, and artistic development. Finally, *Section 5* provides a bibliographical guide to other primary and secondary sources of further reading, among which full details will be found of works cited elsewhere under short titles, and of collected editions of the plays — but not of individual titles, particulars of which will be found with the other factual data in Section 2.

The 'Writer-Files' hope by striking this kind of balance between information and a wide range of opinion to offer 'companions' to the study of major playwrights in the modern repertoire — not in that dangerous pre-digested fashion which can too readily quench the desire to read the plays themselves, nor so prescriptively as to allow any single line of approach to predominate, but rather to encourage readers to form their own judgements of the plays in a wide-ranging context.

Dario Fo was virtually unknown to the English-speaking theatre until around a decade ago: and one of the values of the present volume is that it serves to remind us of how relatively few of his plays have actually crossed the divide — both cultural and linguistic — which makes the style of his work perhaps even less familiar than its content. Instructively, then, we are reminded here that Fo stresses his descent less from the tradition of Commedia dell'Arte — which at least we've read about in our history books — than from the oral tradition of itinerant medieval minstrelsy. The style of performance thus suggested — probably more likely to be found in England in a working men's club than in the West End — has then to address itself to an Italian socio-political scene still heavily dominated by the Catholic Church and subversively influenced by the Mafia: so it is perhaps surprising that we have got to know him at all, still less that *Accidental Death of an Anarchist* and *Can't Pay? Won't Pay!* should figure among the greatest comic hits of both the 'alternative' *and* the commercial theatre during the past decade.

There is, properly, much debate over whether it is even desirable that English-speaking middle-class audiences should thus have kissed the hand that bites the Italian bourgeoisie. Has it been the necessity to adapt his scripts and fill them with native gags that blunts their edge — or the apparent inability of most English and American actors to find an appropriate performance style? One suspects that if the British acting tradition had been shaped by Ben Jonson rather than by Shakespeare, we would have found Fo less problematic. Then, we might have accorded to satirical comedy at least some of the seriousness with which we dignify the tragic mode, and have found it less surprising that a clown should pronounce with political and moral conviction astride outrageously farcical vehicles. It should, of course, also be remembered that, at the level of performance skills, these 'vehicles' include such gems of 'pure' comic theatricality as his invention or (as he would say) rediscovery of 'grammelot' — while at the level of writerly craftsmanship they reveal a pervasive concern with the element of storytelling in drama, which has made Fo's work 'epic' in ways that fuse the Aristotelian and the Brechtian senses of that term. Very properly, this volume also stresses the contribution (on occasion the dominant contribution) of Franca Rame, and reveals Fo's own increasing concern with feminist issues: as ever, when issue fuses with form, that 'bite' is sharp and sure.

Simon Trussler

lifelong atheist, Marxist – sometimes with CP

1926. 24 March, Dario Fo born in San Giano, in the province of Varese, near Lake Maggiore in Lombardy, northern Italy. Eldest child of Felice Fo, an employee of the railways and member of the Socialist Party, and Pina Rota, from a peasant family.

1929. Franca Rame born in Lombardia, and makes her theatrical debut in her mother's arms at the age of eight in her family's travelling theatre troupe. 'All the political arguments which Dario and I have developed had already been put into practice by my family 100 years ago. They "immersed" themselves in every town they toured. My grandfather, father and uncle Tommasso arrived in a city or a town, informed themselves about the history of the place, and then put it on stage.' (Franca Rame, *Domenica del Corriere*, 26 Sept. 1981, p. 61.)

1940. Fo moves to Milan to study art at the Brera Art College. He starts improvising stories and sketches, influenced by the *fabulatori*, or travelling story tellers, around Lake Maggiore.

1942 War breaks out. Fo helps his father in the Resistance, and deserts from the army.

1944 Fo writes his first (unperformed) play, *A Master Drives a Servant Mad, Then the Servant Drives the Master Mad*.

1945-51 Fo returns to Milan and studies set design at the Brera Academy, and architecture at the Milan Polytechnic. Organizes a fake visit to Milan by Picasso. Leaves before completing seven of the final examinations required for a degree.

1948 Rame moves to Milan and performs in a number of variety shows, films and revues.

1949 Fo directs, designs and performs in his farce *But the Tresa Divides Us*, in Luino.

1950 Fo suffers a nervous breakdown, and is advised by a doctor to pursue a career he enjoys. Approaches the actor Franco Parenti, and takes part in his touring outdoor variety show.

1951 Fo's solo radio series, *Poor Dwarf*, transmitted. He takes part in *Seven Days in Milan*, a summer revue with the Nava Sisters, where he meets Franca Rame.

'throw-away theatre' (Fo)

1952 Fo performs *Poor Dwarf* at the Teatro Odeon in Milan. Acts in the revue *Cocorico* with Giustino Durano.

1953 Fo forms The Stand-Ups (I Dritti) with Parenti and Durano. Their satirical revue *A Finger in the Eye*, with lighting by Giorgio Strehler and choreography by Jacques Lecoq, breaks box office records.

1954 Fo and Rame are married. The Stand-Ups' second revue, *A Madhouse for the Sane*, runs into censorship problems and the group disbands. Fo and Rame move to Rome to work in the cinema. *film*

1955 Fo and Rame's son Jacopo born.

1956 Fo writes and acts with Rame in *The Screwball*, directed by Carlo Lizzani, and collaborates on other film screenplays, while Rame acts in a number of films. *film*

1958 The Compagnia Fo-Rame is formed in Milan, and *Thieves, Dummies and Naked Women* opens at the Piccolo Teatro.

59-67 **1959** *Comic Finale* based on plays performed by Rame's family. Fo's 'bourgeois period' begins with *Archangels Don't Play Pinball* at the Teatro Odeon.

1960-61 *He Had Two Pistols with White and Black Eyes* and *Stealing a Foot Makes You Lucky in Love* performed at the Teatro Odeon. *Archangels Don't Play Pinball* is Fo's first play to be produced outside Italy.

1962 Fo appointed artistic director of the popular TV programme *Who's Seen It?* and writes sketches and songs for the TV variety programme *Canzonissima*, watched by 15 million spectators. Fo and Rame terminate their involvement with Italian TV for a period of 15 years after refusing to accept censors' cuts.

1963 *Isabella, Three Sailing Ships and a Con Man* tours Italy. Fo and Rame are attacked by fascists in Rome, Fo is challenged to a duel by a cavalry officer, and the play is charged with slander against the Italian armed forces.

1964 *Seventh Commandment: Thou Shalt Steal a Bit Less* performed in 51 cities in Italy. Fo is the most widely performed Italian playwright in Europe.

1965 *Always Blame the Devil* tours Italy, Europe and Scandinavia.

1966 Fo directs *I Think Things Out and Sing about Them* with Il Nuovo Canzoniere Italiano. Travels to Eastern Europe, the USA and Cuba.

end of 'bourgeois period'

1967 Fo adapts and directs George Michel's play A *Sunday Walk.* *Throw the Lady Out*, a satire on America, is the last play of the 'bourgeois period', and the Compagnia Fo-Rame disbands. 'We were fed up with being the court jesters of the bourgeoisie, on whom our criticism acted like an alka-seltzer, so we decided to become the court jesters of the proletariat.' (Chiara Valentini, *La Storia di Dario Fo*, p. 8.)

1968 Nuova Scena formed, operating through ARCI, the Cultural and Recreational Division of the Italian Communist Party. *Grand Pantomime with Flags and Small and Middle-Sized Puppets* performed in community centres, labour halls and workers' clubs.

1969 First performance of Fo's one-man show *Mistero Buffo*, inspired by the Medieval *jongleurs*, and still in his repertoire. Rame performs in *The Worker Knows 300 Words, the Boss Knows 1,000 — That's Why He's the Boss* and *Chain Me Up and I'll Still Smash Everything*, plays which criticize the Communist Party and lead to a split between the party and Nuova Scena. First American production of Fo's work — *Not All Burglars Have Bad Intentions* and *Marcolfa*, directed by Maurice Edwards at the Cubicolo, Off Broadway.

1970 Fo and Rame form the Colletivo Teatrale La Comune. *I'd Die Tonight If I Didn't Think It Had Been Worth It*, a comparison between Italian partisans and Palestinian freedom fighters, performed in La Comune's new space, the Capannone di via Colletta. This is followed by *Accidental Death of an Anarchist*, 'a grotesque farce about a tragic farce', written in response to audience demands for a play about the 1969 Piazza Fontana bombs in Milan, the 'defenestration' of the anarchist Pino Pinelli, and the repressive, state-orchestrated 'strategy of tension' against the Italian Left.

1971 *United We Stand! All Together Now! Oops! Isn't That the Boss?* is followed by political documentaries about the Communist Party and Palestine.

1972 La Comune evicted from Via Colletta. *Knock Knock! Who's There? Police!*, a sequel to *Accidental Death of an Anarchist*, closes at the Cinema Rossini after the owners refuse to extend the lease due to police pressure. Rame starts Red Aid, a support group for prisoners, and Fo and Rame are subjected to a judicial investigation for allegedly 'subversive' activities.

1973 Rame is abducted and beaten up by a group of fascists. La Comune perform *Down with the Fascists!* Fo is arrested and imprisoned in Sassari, Sardinia, for refusing to allow police to enter a club performance of *The People's War in Chile*. La Comune splits up.

[handwritten margin note at top: turning things upside down: death of an Anarchist — a maniac gets into a police station + puts the police on trial, reversing the process]

1974 'Il Colletivo La Comune diretto da Dario Fo' occupies a disused vegetable market in Milan, the Palazzino Liberty, and performs *We Won't Pay! We Won't Pay!*

1975 *Fanfani Kidnapped*, a political burlesque performed for the election. Fo is nominated as a candidate for the Nobel Prize and visits China.

1976 *Mother's Marijuana is the Best* deals with the drug problem in Italy as 'a class problem: rich people use and consume drugs, while poor people are used and consumed by drugs'. (Valentini, p. 167.)

1977 Fo and Rame return to Italian TV in a retrospective of seven plays transmitted on Channel 2 of RAI, including *Let's Talk about Women*, which later develops into Franca Rame's one-woman show *All House, Bed and Church*. The transmission of *Mistero Buffo* provokes an outraged response from the Vatican, who describe it as 'the most blasphemous show in the history of television'.

1978 Fo is the most widely performed Italian playwright outside Italy. He adapts and directs Stravinsky's *A Soldier's Tale* with students at La Scala. Performs *Tale of a Tiger*, his second one-man show. *We Can't Pay! We Won't Pay!* is Fo's first play to be performed in Britain.

1979 *The Tragedy of Aldo Moro* abandoned after a rehearsed reading. *The End of the World*, written in 1963, is performed in Rome. Fo and Rame perform in Germany, Sweden and Denmark.

1980 *[handwritten margin note: refused entry to U.S.]* Fo and Rame refused visas to enter the USA, allegedly because of their involvement in Red Aid. 'An Evening without Dario Fo and Franca Rame' is held in New York and attended by a number of prominent American writers and intellectuals. *Buona sera con Franca Rame* transmitted on Italian TV. *Accidental Death of an Anarchist* begins a two-year run in London's West End.

1981 *[handwritten margin note: awards: Denmark]* *Hooters, Trumpets and Raspberries* tours Italy. Fo receives the Danish Sonning Prize and the New York Other Critics' Circle Award. *The Opera of Guffaws*, Fo's adaptation of Brecht's *Threepenny Opera*, commissioned but rejected by the Berliner Ensemble, and opens in Prato. *Female Parts* performed at London's National Theatre.

1982 Fo performs his third one-man show, *The Obscene Fable*. Rame performs *All House, Bed and Church* (*Female Parts*) at the Riverside Studios in London. Fo and Rame hold seminars at the Free University of Alcatraz, organized by Jacopo Fo in San Cristina di Gubbio.

1983 *[handwritten margin note: U.S. again]* The clown show *Patapumfete* performed by the Colombaioni brothers. Fo and Rame refused entry visas to the USA for the second time, but perform in London and hold the Riverside workshops.

10

1984 Fo and Rame perform at the Edinburgh Festival and in London (Fo with *The History of Masks*). Fo holds performance-seminars *The Tricks of The Trade* at the Teatro Argentina in Rome. *Dario Fo: The Theatre of the Eye*, an exhibition of videos, costumes, puppets, masks, paintings and drawings by Fo, tours Italy. *Accidental Death of an Anarchist* opens on Broadway, and Fo and Rame are permitted to enter the USA to see it. *Elizabeth* performed in Northern Italy. *Trumpets and Raspberries* opens in London's West End. *The True Story of Piero Angera, Who Wasn't at the Crusades*, originally written in 1960, produced by the Teatro Stabile of Genoa. Fo writes an unperformed play about the Mafia, *God Makes Them and Then Matches Them*. Rame edits *Don't Tell Me about Arches, Tell Me about Your Prisons*

1985 *The Tricks of the Trade* transmitted on Italian TV. *Hellequin, Arlekin, Arlecchino* performed at the Venice Biennale and throughout Italy. Fo is awarded the 'Biglietto d'Oro' (Golden Ticket) at the Taormina Theatre Festival. 'The criterion wasn't audience figures but box office takings; we've always had a policy of very low ticket prices, because we want a popular audience. Even under those conditions they had to give us the prize.' (Fo, in *Europeo*, 19 Oct. 1985, p. 66.)

1986 Fo and Rame embark on a successful tour of the eastern states of the USA with *Mistero Buffo* and *Female Parts*. Rame performs *Open Couple* at the Edinburgh festival and *A Day Like Any Other* in Italy.

1987 Fo directs Rossini's *Barber of Seville* for the Amsterdam Musiktheater. Rame announces in a television interview that she is divorcing him. She tours Italy with *The Kidnapping of Francesca*. Fo publishes *A Shorter Manual for the Actor*, and Fo and Rame direct *Archangels Don't Play Pinball* at the American Repertory Theater in Cambridge, Massachusetts. Rame performs *An Open Couple*, *The Rape* and *Medea* in San Francisco. Fo is offered a Chair in Drama at Rome University. His performance of 'The First Miracle of the Infant Jesus' on an Italian Christmas TV show provokes hundreds of complaints.

1988 Fo performs 'The Lion's Share' (La parte del leone) at the Teatro Metropolitan in Palermo in January: 'a free-wheeling talk-show containing performed monologues chosen, as it were, at random from my twenty-year-long repertoire of *Mistero Buffo*, *Tale of a Tiger* and *The Obscene Fable*. The decision to choose one piece rather than another will be based on the atmosphere created each evening'. (Fo, in *Il Piccolo* (Trieste), 2 Jan. 1988.) Fo and Rame perform in an eight-part TV variety show, *Forced Transmission*. Fo acts in Stefano Benni's film *Music for Old Animals*, his first film role since 1957.

a: Stage Plays

A Finger in the Eye

A revue in two acts by Franco Parenti, Dario Fo and
Giustino Durano.
First production: Piccolo Teatro, Milan, June 1953 (dir. by the
authors).

*A satirical history of the world in 21 sketches. In a
blackout, an actor bangs his head against the wall and
shouts 'lights!' to represent the creation of the world.
The construction of Cheops' pyramids is shown as a
sacrifice of the lives of the slaves who built them. The
Trojan horse is shown to be the idea of an unknown
soldier, but Ulysses gets the credit. The battle between
the Horatians and Curatians is presented as a baseball
match, with a commentator announcing the deaths as
home runs. A Christian is interrogated by the Roman
police in a parody of the prosecution of the
contemporary Italian film critic Guido Aristarco, and
the Crusades are shown to be a colossal exercise in
speculation. Napoleon and Nelson are two little boys
squabbling, the Renaissance originates from a play on
words in an argument between two philosophers, and
the bourgeoisie of the Risorgimento are seen to use the
same language and terminology as the post-war
Christian Democrats' rhetoric against the Italian left.
In the second part, there are satires of American films,
sentimental Italian songs about mothers (parodying the
recently-established San Remo song festival), post-war
building speculation and the legacy of the Krupp
family. The Americans attempt unsuccessfully to go to
the moon, and an expedition climbing the Himalayas
discovers Giulio Andreotti at the top. Finally, the
actors take photos of the audience as if they were at
the zoo.*

The secret to persuasion and entertainment lies in an ability to examine the reality before our eyes by putting a 'finger in the eye', or turning moral interpretations upside down.

> Programme note, 1953, quoted in Claudio Meldolesi,
> *Su un comica in rivolta*, p. 38

The importance, and the novelty, of *A Finger in the Eye* was the fact that it was the first critical revue in Italy, and that it pursued a satirical line that was rigorous rather than whimsical and frothy, in attacking certain aspects of our mores and particularly our culture. Its importance lay in presenting an anti-academic angle on areas dominated by the historical, cultural and social traditions of academicism.

> Morando Morandini, *Sipario*, June 1954, p. 9-10

We didn't give it a precise label, but naturally it was soon referred to as cabaret. Its synthesis of situations, range of subject matter, fragmentary scenes and musical interludes were like cabaret, but we would prefer to call it revue or *avanspettacolo* [see below], which are the two theatrical genres which have developed in Italy in the absence of a cabaret tradition. Naturally we went beyond the normal notion of revue, which was notable for its lack of political commitment and an artificial linear unity. Our linear unity came from a satirical critique of every conceivable subject.

> Dario Fo, in Roberto Mazzucco, *L'avventura del cabaret*, 1976

Avanspettacolo: began in about 1930. A very popular performance genre consisting of brief sketches, songs and various acts. These shows, which lasted about an hour, were performed in the interval at film screenings.

> Dario Fo, *Manuale minimo dell'attore*, 1987, p. 327

Fo's first 'serious' play ... was immediately referred to as an anti-revue. From the moment the curtain went up it was a shock for the audience. The innovation of its staging was so incredibly different from the sumptuous, overblown costumes and millionaire-type sets of normal revues. The acting was dominated by mime, pratfalls, and acrobatic leaps and bounds. Its content was non-conformist, and political satire that was intelligent rather than clumsy and trivial made its first appearance on the post-war Italian stage.

> Chiara Valentini, *La storia di Dario Fo*, 1977, p. 39

13

A Madhouse for the Sane

A revue in two acts by Franco Parenti, Dario Fo and Giustino Durano.
First production: Piccolo Teatro, Milan, 19 June 1954 (dir. by the
authors).

---

*Twenty-four scenes about life in a big city from dawn till dusk,
from the point of view of the underdogs: tramps, thieves, the un-
employed, prisoners, factory workers and lovers. A sketch
satirizing newspapers' manipulation of public opinion shows a
foreign correspondent working from his armchair at home,
while rich society women organize works for charity to alleviate
their boredom, but end up eating all the minestrone they have
made for the local tramps. In 'The Compromise', a dissident
Soviet scientist asks his son to kill him as punishment for his
deviation, and the director of the story, which is being filmed,
appeals for the approval of the censors. A man applying for a
factory job is subjected to a severe psychological test, and
workers sing a song parodying the monotony of the production
line. A worker on a bus has only a ten thousand lire note, which
the conductor refuses to change; other workers on the bus club
together to change the note, at which point the conductor offers
to change the note and reimburse them. There are satires of film
buffs and government initiatives to exploit illiteracy and the
mass media.*

... A form of popular theatre ... a collective text ... almost surreal,
recalling the late French decadent poets ... the language is freed by
concrete representations which give a human value to some of the
characters in situations which are synthetic (and at times overloaded).
Salvatore Quasimodo, *Tempo,* 1 July 1954

Thieves, Dummies and Naked Women

Four one-act farces.
First production: Piccolo Teatro, Milan, 6 June 1958. *Corpses Are
Despatched* [sic] transmitted on RAI TV, 3 Feb. 1959, *One Was
Nude and the Other Wore Tails* on 27 Feb. 1962, and *Housepainters*

Have No Memories on 20 March 1962. *Not All Burglars Have Bad
Intentions* revived at Teatro Leopardi, Rome, Oct. 1980
(dir. Marco Lucchesi).
American production: Not All Burglars Have Bad Intentions at
Cubicolo, New York, Aug. 1969 (trans. and dir. Maurice Edwards).
Australian productions: Corpses are Despatched ... Flinders
University, Adelaide, 1972 (trans. B. Fennario), *Every Burglar has
Silver Lining* at Seymour Centre, Sydney, Aug. 1981
(trans. Tim Fitzpatrick, dir. Mick Rodger).

Not All Burglars Have Bad Intentions *is a 'pochade' about a
burglar who is surprised in the act of robbing a house by the
owner and his mistress. The burglar's wife rings him 'at work'
and becomes jealous of the other woman. Then the owner's wife
arrives with her lover, and in the ensuing complications the
burglar manages to escape.* One Was Nude and the Other Wore
Tails *is a 'musical farce' about an Ambassador who is forced to
flee when he is discovered by his mistress's husband, and is
found naked in a street sweeper's cart. The street sweeper
becomes involved in a complicated ploy to obtain a dinner suit
for him.* Housepainters Have No Memories *is a 'clown farce' in
which two men impersonating housepainters discover the
woman of the house's lover has been embalmed by his jealous
wife, and in the belief that they have caused his death, set off a
series of disguises and mistaken identities. In* Women Undressed
and Bodies to be Despatched, *a 'thriller farce', a transvestite
detective investigates a woman who is running a divorce agency,
which is a cover for a human mincemeat factory.*

These farces were an important exercise for me in writing texts for the
theatre. I learned how to dismantle and re-assemble the mechanisms of
comedy, and write directly for the stage without any literary
intermediary. I also realized how many antiquated, useless things there
were in many plays which belonged to the theatre of words.

Fo, 1977, in Valentini, p. 58

I realized conclusively that all real theatre is theatre of situation. Every
theatrical action arises from a situation on stage which is full of
possibilities for developing the action. The dialogue is only one of the
tools to express these developments. For example: a naked man hides in

15

an empty street sweeper's cart. This is already a situation; when the street sweeper discovers him, an innumerable series of situations can develop from the first situation. Theatre based on autonomous dialogue developing action which doesn't express potential action isn't theatre, it's literature. Theatrical language is synthetic, and can't accommodate descriptive digressions about states of mind, unless they are part of the momentum one wishes to sustain.

Fo, in Erminia Artese, *Dario Fo parla di Dario Fo*, 1977, p. 22

A taste for paradox, misunderstanding, absurdity and surrealism is expressed by making maximum use of stagecraft. Thus the often-expressed parallel between Fo's 'surrealism' and the Theatre of the Absurd (Ionesco and Adamov are most often cited) breaks down. ... The satirical barbs of the two earlier works have disappeared ... and the staging has moved from innovation to a naturalism with grotesque ramifications.

Marina Cappa and Roberto Nepoli, *Dario Fo*, 1982, p. 39-40

Comic Finale

Four one-act farces.

First production: Teatro Stabile, Turin, 10 Dec. 1958 (dir. Fo and Gian Franco De Bosio). *Corpse for Sale* transmitted RAI TV, 20 Feb. 1962, and *Marcolfa* on 6 March 1962.

British production: Corpse for Sale, Derby Playhouse, Apr. 1986 (trans. Ed Emery; dir. Claire Grove).

American and Canadian productions: Marcolfa at Cubicolo Theatre, New York, August 1969, *Corpse for Sale* at New Theatre '83, University of Windsor, Ontario, Canada, 15 June 1983 (trans. Walter Temelini).

In When You're Poor You'll Be King, *based on the carnival 'feast of fools', a group of strolling players dissuade an old man from his belief that he will become king if he squanders all his money and becomes a pauper.* Marcolfa *updates the Commedia dell'Arte character who is the mother of Bertoldo into the servant who is courted by everyone in an aristocratic household after she wins the lottery, but opts for her good-for-nothing fiancé. In* Corpse for Sale, *some card sharks kill a simpleton after he beats them at cards, and then discover that he is a dangerous criminal. The dead man revives and marries the*

16

landlord's daughter. The Three Suitors *revolves around a mis-understanding between three daughters of a wealthy landowner and three 'ghostbusters' he employs to rid his castle of evil spirits, whom the daughters take for suitors.*

Fo has revived an almost extinct comic vitality and retraced its origins, finding clear historical links with contemporary society. He has used the scenarios ... performed by one of the most outstanding nineteenth-century comic family troupes, the Rame family of Piedmont. ... He has retained the essential aspects ... but embellished them with a completely new succession of situations, extending and multiplying the surprises ... with a completely modern freedom of invention.

Giorgio Guazzotti, *Il Dramma*, Nov. 1958, p. 59

Because of this unusual mixture of popular and high cultural elements, and an attempt to combine the refined lessons of mime and the French avant-garde with the gags of the nineteenth-century *guitti*, the *lazzi* [see below] of the Commedia dell'Arte, circus tricks and Brechtian anti-naturalism into a single theatrical form, the critics found themselves in a dilemma: were Dario Fo's plays vaudeville, pochades, a new kind of revue, or avant-garde theatre? Probably this confusion was the greatest strength and popularity of a type of theatre which had too much vitality to be labelled easily.

Valentini, 1977, p. 60

Guitto: actor from a travelling theatre company of the lowest order, the so-called 'mountain climbers'. An expression used pejoratively to describe an actor who performs without care or discrimination, without taking any care over make-up or costumes.

Fo, *Manuale minimo dell'attore*, 1987, p. 337

Lazzi: the most ancient form of 'improvisation'. The scenarios of the Commedia dell'Arte are literally crammed with the expression 'lazzi' or 'lazzo'. It means a comic device, either mimed or verbal, which is almost never described. The way in which the scenarios developed was never written down in order to pass on the various theatrical devices to others who did not belong to the companies. For the actors in the Commedia companies they served exclusively as memos, and they preferred to keep the development of the comic details and grotesque devices to themselves, virtually secret.

As above, p. 338

17

Political commitment took a back seat for a while. These plays were primarily devices to make people laugh, although a populist subtext was already detectable; a popular nose-thumbing at the rich and powerful.

Gian Franco De Bosio, in Valentini, p. 59

Archangels Don't Play Pinball

Three-act play, partly based on a short story by Augusto Frassineti.
First production: Teatro Odeon, Milan, 11 Sept. 1959 (dir. Fo).
British production: BBC Radio 3, May 1986 (adapt. and
    dir. James Runcie; trans. R. C. McAvoy and A. M. Giugni); Bristol
    Old Vic, 10 Sept. 1986 (dir. Glen Walford).
American production: America Repertory Th., Cambridge, Mass.,
    5 Jan. 1987 (trans. Ron Jenkins; dir. Fo and Rame).
Australian production: University of New South Wales, Sydney,
    2 Sept. 1986 (trans. and dir. Tony Mitchell).

A group of young Milanese petty criminals play a trick on one of their number, Stretch, a modern version of the clever fool Bertoldo, and marry him off to a fake Albanian beauty (who is actually a prostitute) in a mock marriage ceremony. Stretch then tries to get his identity papers so that he can draw a disability pension, only to find that he has been registered as a hunting dog, a bureaucratic error he can only rectify by going to a kennel and posing as a dog. The play follows his attempts to extricate himself from the desperate demi-monde of pranks and petty crime, get his papers in order, and find an identity for himself. This includes impersonating a politician whose trousers he steals on a train, and re-encountering the prostitute, who is posing as the politician's wife. At the end, he discovers everything has been a dream, although not manipulated as he thought by the archangels in a game of human pinball.

If it weren't for the liberal dose of madness he possesses, Fo would be a preacher, a moralist. Luckily for him (and us) he is a preaching clown. Farce represents a tool of moral corrosiveness for him, which by its very nature provides a pretext for escapism and paradoxical exercises. ... But here all the congenial acrobatics of farce are rediscovered, along with some pointed references to reality.

Ghigo De Chiara, *Sipario*, Sept 1959, p. 37

The play contains two clearly heterogeneous elements: the nucleus comes from a Frassineti story with its typical fantastical-satirical romantic humour. Bureaucracy becomes a symbol of modern technocracy and its oppressive hierarchy is mocked. The combination of Fo and Frassineti in the second act result in the most evocative and distinctive moments of the play, embodied in exhilaratingly crazy set pieces in which Fo reveals his ability to turn contemporary reality upside down and show its underbelly. The rest of the play is made up of witty comic turns which are artfully sustained by his *brio*.

Vito Pandolfi, *Storia del teatro drammatico*, 1962

I took the starting point of the play from current events, and the paradoxical contradictions of the Christian Democrat state, and I took the subject into areas which would clash with audiences on the commercial circuit. Having accepted this circuit and these audiences, we had to put across political and social truths in the guise of satiric licence. ... The play was performed with the same rhythm as a film, where scenes and events followed a cinematic kind of sequence — even the locations changed continually; at least ten times — as in a film.

Fo, in Valentini, 1977, p. 64, 66

... Genial but toothless. ... What Fo is doing is clear: drawing on popular Italian culture, including the Harlequin and Columbine story, while at the same time aiming a few swipes at the chicanery, corruption, nepotism and time-wasting form-filling of his native land. But Fo's good nature swamps the social and political protest.

Michael Billington, *The Guardian*, 17 Sept. 1986

... A collector's item ... though it is not explicitly political. ... Instead of satirizing actual cases of terrorism or police corruption, *Archangels* offers a generalized farcical world of haves and have-nots. ... It is a wonderful piece of theatrical legerdemain and also a defiant gesture in which you can read the future author of *Can't Pay? Won't Pay!*

Irving Wardle, *The Times*, 21 Sept. 1986

Technically it is a quick-moving farce which draws on some of the classic situations of the French tradition of Labiche and Feydeau, with bedroom confusions and pompous officialdoms. Its use of the transformation of the hero into an animal looks further back to the literature of the Roman Empire — to the story of Apuleis and his golden ass, who suffered the same fate. The intervention of the archangels at the end is an irresistible reminder of the *deus ex machina* of classical theatre and an interesting parallel to the part played by the gods in Brecht's *Good Person of Szechwan*. ... The social provenance of the characters is also unusual. The young men in what one might call their 'real life' sequences — for the bulk of the play is a dream — are youths from the sub-proletariat who recall the wide boys Pasolini describes in his novels set in the working-class suburbs of Rome. Their butt is Lofty, a simple young man who describes himself as 'the Rigoletto of the poor' — as, in fact, a *giullare*, [*see below*] the innocent who by his literal reading of situations reveals them in all their absurdity.

Stuart Hood, 'Introduction' to Fo, *Archangels Don't Play Pinball*, Methuen, 1987, p. xiv-xv

Giullare: medieval actor, acrobat and juggler of distinctly popular origins. The *giullari* performed in taverns, piazzas, courtyards and were often invited into the courts of the gentry and princes. On special occasions they also performed in churches.

Fo, *Manuale*, p. 336

He Had Two Pistols with White and Black Eyes

Three-act play.
First production: Teatro Odeon, Milan, 2 Sept. 1960 (dir. Fo).
British production: Sherman Centre, Cardiff, 1985 (as *Two Pistols*, trans. Katie Dymoke).

An (allegedly false) victim of amnesia is in a psychiatric institution, dressed in a priest's cassock. He meets Luisa, who recognizes him as her old lover who has gone to the war, and takes him home with her. The amnesiac does not recognize either the home or the lifestyle the woman explains were his; instead of the harsh and arrogant man she expected, he is docile and full of remorse for the past. Meanwhile the real 'gent', the roguish Giovanni Gallina, returns; the other man is merely his double. There is a series of misunderstandings and mistaken identities, until the crook discovers the confusion and decides to hold the amnesiac priest prisoner. Giovanni resumes his life of crime, flees from a police ambush and appears to have caused the death of his double at the hands of the police, who think he is Gallina. He organizes a thieves' strike, demanding a percentage of the advantages which upstanding members of the community (insurance companies, dog trainers, crime reporters ...) gain from their thefts. Luisa discovers that the coordinator of the strike is not Giovanni (as the gang of thieves had assumed) but the amnesiac. He is about to be arrested for impersonating a priest when he is recognized by the director of a prison rehabilitation centre as his beloved Don Filippo.

Cappa and Nepoli, p. 49-50

Its intentions are very clear but not fully realized, and the play becomes stodgy and monotonous at times where it could have been fast and entertaining. ... Fo's favourite gags, although amusing, are too dominant, fragment the dialogue and prevent any real development of the characters and events. ... Nonetheless highly enjoyable and at times irresistible.

Roberto Rebora, *Sipario*, Oct 1960, p. 25

... Resembles Brecht's *Threepenny Opera* which had just been staged by Strehler at the Piccolo Teatro, and is a kind of gangster story, a black comedy based on an exchange of personalities — a fascist bandit and a Christian Democrat priest. ... The jibes at authority were clear from the moment the curtain went up ...

Valentini, p. 70-1

... Satirized latent Fascism. It was the story of a bandit whose two-sided character was portrayed through the use of doubles, in the tradition of Greek and Roman theatre. Censorship had become just about intolerable, and we almost ended in jail for having refused to submit the text for approval by the authorities, knowing that permission could be obtained only after they mutilated the work beyond all recognition.

'Dario Fo Explains: an Interview with
Luigi Ballerini and Giuseppe Risso', 1978, p. 46

He Who Steals a Foot is Lucky in Love

Two-act play.
First production: Teatro Odeon, Milan, 8 Sept. 1961 (dir. Fo). *Revived* at
Teatro Belli, Rome, 25 Jan. 1987 (dir. Antonio Salines).

He Who Steals a Foot is Lucky in Love

British production: Channel 5 Theatre, Glasgow, 11 Aug. 1983
(trans. Helen Russell).

A thief (Apollo) and aspiring taxi driver steals the foot of a statue of Mercury from a museum with an accomplice, and buries it in the ground where a construction company is building, in order to blackmail the owner of the firm. The fraud is successful — the two thieves disguise themselves as archaeologists and turn up at the construction company. They are given three million lire to keep quiet and not obstruct the works. Apollo buys a taxi, and meets the wife of the boss of the construction company (Daphne). ... She offers him money to pretend that he has been involved in a car accident with her, in order to hide a nose operation from her husband. When he arrives home, the building contractor does not recognize the fake archaeologist, but assumes he is having an affair with Daphne — permissible in their social class. A series of misunderstandings culminates in the arrival of a doctor, who pronounces that the woman is suffering from a mortal illness which is curable by continuous blood transfusions between her and the taxi driver, who is the only person with the same blood group. This 'medical' union between them ... continues ... because Apollo pretends to be pregnant with Daphne's child. The husband ... demands a divorce, and the love story ... is interrupted by her escape (since happiness is impossible between people of such different social classes). She is substituted with the mythical plant (Daphne, or laurel), which Apollo embraces affectionately.

Cappa and Nepoli, p. 52

... A collection of little inventions — stealing the foot and planting it on the two building speculators is more of an apology, really. In a sense it is the play that comes closest to our 'revues', because the main thread of the story is very thin — a pretext for a series of barbs against the authorities of the time.

Fo, in Artese, p. 46

Fo returns to one of his starting points, the *fabulatori*. Consequently the protagonist of this play is an emigrant from the south of Italy who represents a different culture from the sophisticated bourgeois environment of the play. ... The plot is a reworking of the classical myth of Daphnis and Chloe. Formally, it is partly a farce for clowns, and partly a bedroom farce ... it is the only play of Fo's not to use songs, and comes closest to a traditional comic form.

Bent Holm, *The World Turned Upside Down: Dario Fo and the Popular Imagination*, Stockholm, 1980, p. 71-2

Isabella, Three Sailing Ships and a Con Man

Two-act play.
First production: Teatro Odeon, Milan, 6 Sept. 1963 (dir. Fo). TV
    version: transmitted on RAI 2, 11 and 13 May 1977.

An actor (is) condemned to death for acting in a play by Rojas which has been banned. At the gallows he is allowed to perform the story of Christopher Columbus, which he drags out as long as he can in the hope that a pardon will arrive. This does not eventuate, however, and in the end he loses his head. The play about Columbus presents the Genovese hero as an obsessive, wily individual, pitting his wits against Isabella, Filippo, Giovanna the madwoman, the (Spanish) court, sailing ships, enemies, a trial, and eventual obscurity, a consequence of the fact that cunning and unscrupulousness (even to honourable ends) is not enough if the powers that be are not on your side.

Roberto Rebora, *Sipario*, Oct. 1963, p. 28

I wanted to attack those Italian intellectuals who, with the centre-left and the Socialist Party in the government, had discovered power and its advantages, and leaped on it like rats on a piece of cheese. I wanted to dismantle a character who had been embalmed as a hero in school history books, whereas in fact he is an intellectual who tries to keep afloat within the mechanisms of power, play games with the King, and be cunning with power figures, only to end up reduced to a poor sod. I'd started to view the present with the tools of history and culture, in order to assess it better, and in this play I invited the audience to use these tools.

Fo, in Valentini, p. 85

23

Fo's most Brechtian play, in its attempt to reconstruct a character, Columbus, who symbolizes a particular epoch and mentality, in its use of songs which do not merely provide support for the action but function as commentary, and for the careful historical research which lay behind the plot.

Valentini, p. 85

Seventh Commandment: Thou Shalt Steal a Bit Less

Two-act play.
First production: Teatro Odeon, Milan, 4 Sept. 1964 (dir. Fo). TV
    version: transmitted on RAI 2, 6 May 1977.
Australian production: University of Queensland, 1973
    (trans. T. Schonnell).

Enea, a female gravedigger, is persuaded by her colleagues in a practical joke that the cemetery where she works is being demolished by building speculators. She is then convinced she should pursue a vocation as a prostitute, and witnesses a clash between police and striking workers, in which she sympathizes with the police. She encounters a victim of 'coffin mania' who wants to rent a coffin, and discovers that the owner of the cemetery is in fact planning to sell it to speculators. Enea disguises herself as a nun, and infiltrates a mental asylum to obtain compromising documents with which to blackmail people in positions of authority. There she again meets the 'coffin maniac', who promises to help her expose corruption in high places, but in the end, in order to prevent a scandal that would be 'worse than an atomic bomb', everyone is subjected to brainwashing with a trephine, except for Enea, who vows to 'go back where she came from'.

The social satire is more open and direct than in the other plays. Behind the plot and its twists and turns is the most rampant and astonishing building speculation and the impetus of recurrent scandals in Italian politics. ... The bitterness and cruelty are dispersed rather than submerged by the breadth and complexity of imagination which as always in Fo's plays manifests itself in the action and develops continuously without allowing the audience any respite.

Franco Vegliani, *Sipario*, Aug.-Sept. 1964, p. 39

... A successful synthesis of all the 'values' of [Fo's] theatre: an almost perfectly balanced farcical mechanism, comic poise and clever mime, ironic impulse and satirical flights of fancy ... achieving by its continual and inexorable inventiveness a kind of 'chain reaction' which appears to be governed by a rigorous necessity. ... Lively, bold and generous ... the language is both popular, due to the the presence of dialect, and highly proficient in its cultured comic effects (puns, assonance, etc.)

Arturo Lazzari, *L'Unita*, 5 Sept. 1964

There are two main starting points; a cemetery about to be demolished because a group of speculators have bought up all the buildings around it and want to remove the unpleasant view for their tenants, and a bank vault in a psychiatric institution run by nuns who subject the patients to electroshock therapy twice a day. The nuns also make them vote for the Christian Democrats and teach them 'current beliefs' like telling jokes about unimportant ministers and even priests can calm their nerves, that they may talk about prices and taxes being too high, but that going on strike is wrong because it makes the pope angry, that [the state] sends all its petty cash off to Switzerland, finances foreign companies who don't pay taxes, but is good because it provides work. In the farce that develops around these two basic ideas we put in as many references to corruption as possible. A female character provides the central thread of the story: the play is dedicated to Franca.

Fo, in Artese, p. 47

... The cemetery could be seen ... from the point of view of popular mythology as the 'world of the dead'. In realistic terms, the psychiatric hospital alludes to scandals and corruption in the public sector, symbolically it is a political and satirical image of official society, and from the point of view of popular mythology it is the world of the mad, the universe of demons, where constitutional order is turned upside down in an anarchic, carnivalesque universe.

Bent Holm, p. 233

Always Blame the Devil

Two-act play.
First production: Teatro Odeon, Milan, 10 Sept. 1965 (dir. Fo).

Set at the end of the thirteenth-century, the play is about Amalasunta, a female charlatan who is unjustly accused of being a witch, and decides to become one as a result. She enlists the aid of Brancaleone, a devil-dwarf, and when she is employed for her magical powers in the court of a Duke, he becomes a kind of incubus to her. They both plot to assassinate the Duke, and after they are successful, the Duke's body is made into a marionette by a wizard in order to prevent the people from revolting. But Brancaleone gets inside the body and persuades the members of the Cathar commune to instigate a revolution, so that they will then be killed by the imperial forces, which are about to arrive. As a result Brancaleone becomes the new Duke.

... A farce which brings invisible devils and false witches on to the stage, and manages to attack catholicism as an instrument of power without resorting to parables. The authorities claim that the Gospels are too abrasive to be put into practice and that they are dangerous, because if they were applied they would abolish all their privileges. Some of the songs in the play are based on heretical songs of the time. Clearly we had to expand the boundaries of farce to attack the clergy and religion of the 1960s. ... Unlike *Mistero Buffo* it is not a *giullarata*, or a reconstruction of medieval texts, but a totally invented story in a farcical vein, which takes advantage of its medieval setting to tell a few truths about Catholicism.

Fo, in Artese, *p. 49*

... Almost too rich in inventiveness and somewhat underdeveloped satirical sallies. At the politico-historical kernel of the play is the struggle between the Holy Roman Emperor and the Cathars, the communitarian and evangelic sect wiped out for heresy in the late thirteenth century ... the allegory is obvious. The Cathar communards stand for the Italian communists, the Imperial forces represent the USA which, at the time, was stepping out of its commitment in Vietnam. An interesting pointer to the later Fo is his attempt here to disinter authentically revolutionary episodes from the history of popular culture, especially those involving pre-reformation evangelical religion, which challenges the corrupt and reactionary orthodoxy from an, as it were, left wing point of view.

Lino Pertile, 'Dario Fo', 1984, p. 174

Throw the Lady Out

Two-act play
First production: Teatro Manzoni, Milan, 15 Sept. 1967 (dir. Fo).
   TV version: transmitted on RAI 2, 9 and 11 Nov. 1976.

*A clown show satirizing America, personified by 'the Lady', and
presented as a battle between two rival circuses. A religious
ceremony centred on a refrigerator opens the show, which is a
series of disconnected sketches which were updated and
changed for the 1976 TV version of the play. The Lady is
succeeded by the Bride, who is assassinated at Dallas, where
'Clown Dario' conducts a tortuous ballistic test tracing the
trajectory of the bullet that has killed her, which has hit a stray
dog, a chauffeur and an ice cream van on its way to its target.
There is a trial investigating the murder of Lee Harvey Oswald,
and an inquest into the murder of a black man, interspersed with
circus acts like peeping-tom clowns and a flea trainer who has
to have the appendix of one of his fleas removed. In another
sketch, unborn children are conscripted into the army, and their
mothers sent to Vietnam, where orders are transmitted by
telephone into the mothers' stomachs. Fo also added a
celebrated sketch in which he plays Saint George as a dwarf,
riding a three-metre-high dragon which symbolized imperialism.*

... A highly proficient clown show, in which the circus device assumes a
complex technical, aesthetic and narrative function. ... He has avoided
giving his clowns poetic, symbolic or metatheatrical significance, as
playwrights and directors who draw on circus devices often do. ... This
clown show becomes political theatre, preserving a balance which only
rarely topples (at times in the second act it lapses into didacticism). ...
For the freshness of its invention, its sense of pace and timing ... its use
of 'distanced' farcical and grotesque devices, and especially for its
biting references to social and political issues, it recalls the far-off days
of *A Finger in the Eye*, although it is undoubtedly superior, more mature,
polished and assured ...

                              Arturo Lazzari, *L'Unita*, 16 Sept. 1967

Set in an American circus of the 1860s ... progressed like a circus performance: acrobats, clowns, dancers, tightrope walkers, and trapeze artists rushed on and off. A hundred mechanical contraptions whirred and hummed. the pace was frenetic; the joy excessive, manic. Fo and his company sang, danced, joked, performed on the high wire, executed impressive feats of acrobatics. His verbal banter, spiced with his Milanese argot, delighted the audience, but in the end it was gesture and movement that prevailed over language. Among that gesture and movement were an avalanche of teeth pouring out of Fo's mouth, an oxygen mask that became a serpent, shoes propelled by themselves, hands flying through the air, and performers sitting in mid-air with their coat-tails folded under them, plus an endless array of surrealistic sight gags. Gradually, however, one realized that the joy was fraught with tragedy, clearly evident in the death of a dove at Dallas. The lady to be eliminated was the owner of the circus, an aged female P. T. Barnum, representing American capitalism. A moment before her death, she was elevated above a sink in a Statue of Liberty pose, and then ascended to a heaven packed with consumer goods, a touch of mock ritual denigrating both Church and State. Fo's circus was a metaphor of the industrial state, a vast bureaucracy of machines and trapezes in which man had yielded his individuality to the collective pandemonium, a puppet in a tyrannical circus of injustice, prejudice, crime and war.

> A. Richard Sogliuzzo, 'Dario Fo: Puppets
> for a Proletarian Revolution', 1972, p. 73

… There were real clowns in it — the Colombaioni (Alberto, Charlie and Ramono, and Alberto's wife, an acrobat) — and I had to employ various effects and breakneck acrobatic tricks, explosions, trapeze acts, walking on springy stilts, and falling vertically into a dustbin. The Colombaioni know how to perform these to perfection, and taught us a lot of other tricks which weren't in the script. I've learned almost everything I know of and about clowns from them, including how to play the trombone. Franca learned how to work on a trapeze and do falls, hanging from her feet with her legs crossed. Because of the vast range and complexity of techniques that a clown has to acquire, it could be said that an actor who picks up this technical know-how is at an enormous advantage … not only in comic roles, but — and I can see the 'armchair' theatre critics shuddering in horror at this — in tragic roles too. … The clown goes back a very long way: clowns existed before the origins of the Commedia dell'Arte. It could be said that the Italian Commedia masks were born from an obscene marriage of female jongleuses, fabulatori and clowns, and then after incestuous relationships, 'Commedia' gave birth to scores of other clowns.

> Fo, *Manuale*, p. 256

Grand Pantomime with Small and Middle-Sized Puppets

Two-act play.
First production: Nuova Scena at Camera di Lavoro, Sala Di Vittorio,
  Milan, Autumn 1968 (dir. Fo). Revised version entitled *Death and
  Resurrection of a Puppet* performed by La Comune, Capannone
  di via Colletta, 4 Dec. 1971 (dir. Fo).

*A giant puppet representing fascism gives birth to a King and
Queen, Capital, the Bourgeoisie, a General, a Bishop, and the
Confederation of Industry. These allegorical figures combat the
revolt of the people, represented by an enormous Chinese
dragon. A bourgeois Dolly Girl seduces the leader of the
Rebels, who succumb to a Wizard who sells them football and
advertising as a means of letting off steam. A television director,
trying to make a powerful documentary about the Russian
invasion of Czechoslovakia, inserts some stock footage from
Vietnam. Prospective factory employees are subjected to a
psychological and political interrogation, and then trained for
an assembly line by a ballet teacher. The Minister of the Interior
is wrongly arrested when he becomes entangled in a student
demonstration during an amorous rendezvous, and the play ends
with a song by Mikis Theodorakis celebrating 'the youth of the
month of May'. In* Death and Resurrection of a Puppet *Fo,
wearing a mask, played PCI leader Palmiro Togliatti, whose
policies were contrasted with those of Lenin and Mao,
represented by puppets. The play attacked the revisionism of the
PCI, American imperialism, and right-wing terrorism.*

Not his best play, but more than any other play it justifies its existence
through its rapport with its audience. ... He is aware of the dangers of
didacticism ... and has attempted, often successfully, to dress his
arguments up in theatrical inventiveness.

                    Ettore Capriolo, *Sipario,* Jan. 1969, p. 43-4

... A political satire of the past quarter of a century of Italian history. It
dealt with the struggle between the proletariat and the bourgeoisie,
which was conveyed primarily through the use of puppets that the actors

moved about on the stage or manipulated with strings or sticks in full view of the audience. The manipulation of puppets by warring political factions became a vivid stage metaphor. The continual presence of the monstrous puppet on stage served as a sinister reminder of the omnipresence of political oppression. ... Many of the masks were based on those of the Roman comedy and the Commedia dell'Arte. The puppets resembled George Grosz cartoons but lacked their horror. Despite the seriousness of the theme, Fo's productions retain the surface charm and magic of children's theatre.

Sogliuzzo, 1972, p. 75-6

When we got involved with ARCI, in was in the hope that the spirit of 1968 was moving things in a new direction, even though we were well aware of what cooperatives involved, and who was behind the *case del popolo* [*Communist Party (PCI) community centres*], and in whose interest they were. We had the illusion that working on a grass roots level, we could change the organizational structures, and that the PCI had adopted a revolutionary line as a result of the pressure of the student and workers' movements. We saw it as the only possible solution, the only representative of the working class.

Fo, 'Per Una nuova gestione degli spazi e degli spettacoli', 1976,
in Franco Quadri, *Il teatro del regime*, p. 143

... Full, perhaps too full, of things left unsaid for many years, lines cut by the censor or self-censored. The play has a wildly comic structure, using a number of elements from popular theatre (masks and Sicilian puppets adapted to a similar theatrical use to what the Bread and Puppet Theatre were doing at the same time in the USA) in an epic set-up, aspects of which recall Brecht's didactic plays. ... It deals with Italy from the resistance to the consumer society, the transformation of the ruling class, and the continuation of many elements of fascism into the new society.

Valentini, p. 12

If, in the simplistic dialectical interplay the play is based on, Togliatti is the thesis, Mao the antithesis, and the victorious dragon the synthesis ... polemic against the party has taken Fo to such an extreme that he doesn't realize the shifting sands he is moving on to. ... And it is a pity, because his power as a popular author and actor comes through even in this play.

Edoardo Fadini, *Rinascita*, 14 Jan 1972

Death and Resurrection of a Puppet attacked revisionism in an unintelligent way ... on an ideological level, and ... stopped at a point of destruction without indicating any constructive way ahead or signs of political re-organization ... enabling revisionists to attack us as anti-communist, and this falsehood gained a certain degree of credibility on a mass level. We took this experience into account in *Law and Order for God and Money's Sake*, where the attack on revisionism was much clearer but less frontal and more deep-seated ...

Document released by La Comune, Sept. 1972,
quoted in Artese, p. 131-2

Grand Pantomime was revived in the 1971-72 season with a lot of revisions, since we realized that it couldn't remain unchanged after 1969 and its struggles for workers' contracts, the 'hot autumn' with its wave of workers' and students' struggles, and the 'state massacres'. The script of the second edition of the play was discussed in an analytical meeting at which the main workers' nuclei of the vanguard of various factories in Milan were present, and there was a second analysis after the first rehearsal. ... There were also puppets of Marcos and Joe Mo' (Stalin). They appeared on the stage of a little theatre where their arguments took place. The little theatre was used to distance these leaders of the people, who were symbols of different ways of conceptualizing relations with the proletariat. ... The history of the years 1943 to 1972 was reconstructed from the point of view of proletarian struggles and every part of the play was viewed from this perspective ... to extend the job of writing a play to a collective means accepting an idea of theatre and its political function which is substantially different from plays by playwrights ...

Fo, in Artese, p. 129-34

Mistero Buffo

A 'giullarata popolare' in fifteenth-century Padano dialect.
First production: Sestri Levanti, 1 Oct. 1969 (dir. Fo). TV version:
    transmitted on RAI 2, 22 and 29 Apr. 18 and 25 Nov. 1977.
British production: Puppet versions (trans. and dir. Malcolm Knight),
    Maskot Puppet Theatre, Glasgow, 15 Aug. 1983; 1982 Theatre
    Company at the Half Moon Theatre, London, Feb. 1984
    (trans. Ed Emery).
Australian productions: Flinders University, Adelaide, 30 Sept. 1987
    (trans. and dir. Antonio Comin); Fringe Club, Adelaide, 2 Mar. 1988
    (trans. Ed Emery; dir. Leonard Kovner).

A series of one-person performance pieces based on Medieval texts originally performed by the giullari. *The 'Hymn of the Flagellants' opens a series of pieces of varying lengths which include 'The Drunkard' (later called 'The Wedding Feast of Canaan') in which a drunken guest present at Christ's miracle of the changing of water into wine recounts the story from a highly Dionysian, irreverent point of view, after chasing away an angel who is trying to tell the official version of the story. In 'The Slaughter of the Innocents' a mad woman has substituted a sheep for her dead baby, and is accosted by a Roman soldier who takes it for a real baby, and then tells her story to the Madonna, who unsuccessfully attempts to console her. In 'The Resurrection of Lazarus', Christ's miracle is narrated by fifteen different characters in the crowd waiting for the miracle, which finally occurs, spraying people with maggots as Lazarus revives, while the final narrator has his pocket picked in mid-sentence. 'Boniface VIII' dresses up in all his papal finery, ordering his altar boys around in a display of fascistic arrogance and vanity. He encounters Christ, who refuses to recognize or acknowledge him as pope, and finally gives him a series of invisible kicks in the backside for his decadence and corruption. The two protagonists of the 'Morality of the Blind Man and the Cripple' join forces in an attempt at self-sufficiency, the cripple riding on the blind man's back, and try unsuccessfully to avoid being 'miracled' by Christ, which will involve having to work and be exploited by a master. 'The Origin of the Underling' relates the creation of a peasant-serf 'from an ass's fart', so that the master can have someone to do his dirty work. The master then proceeds to give the serf religious instruction, teaching him that he is a vulgar, menial and repellent creature, who nonetheless has an eternal soul which will bring him joy and fulfilment in the hereafter. An Angel calls the master's bluff and sows the seeds of a peasants' revolt. There are also four 'Texts from the Passion', starting with 'Death and the Madman', in which a madman draws the tarot card of death in an inn where Christ and the apostles are staying. A female figure of Death arrives, and the Madman seduces her away from her duty. In 'Mary Comes to Know of her Son's Sentence', the Virgin Mary's friends conceal her son's death from her, but she sees the imprint of his face on Veronica's shroud. In 'The Madman beneath the Cross', the protagonist watches the Roman soldiers betting on how many blows it will take to nail Christ up to the cross. He then offers the thirty pieces of silver Judas has thrown away in return for Christ's body. In 'Mary's Passion at the Cross', Mary tries to bargain with the Roman soldiers for her son's body, and is unconvinced by the Archangel Gabriel's attempts to explain the importance of the Crucifixion.*

In later performances, Fo added 'Fresh Fragrant Rose', a discourse on the way popular erotic poetry was censored by clerics and bourgeois scholars and transformed into 'high culture' as courtly love poetry, and 'Zanni's Grammelot', about a starving peasant who is so hungry he imagines eating himself, then dreams of having a gargantuan meal, only to awake to find himself still hungry, and catches and eats a fly. 'The Origin of the Giullare' is the story of a peasant whose wife is raped by a greedy landowner trying to confiscate his land, which he does. About to hang himself, the peasant is visited by Christ, who makes him into a giullare, giving him 'a new language which will cut like a knife'. Three other Grammelots deal with an 'English Lawyer' who saves a nobleman's skin in a rape case by proving that the peasant girl he raped exerted her seductive powers on him, an 'American Technocrat' who presents a potted history of aviation from the Wright brothers to space travel, and 'Scapino's Grammelot', which contains instructions to an actor about how to impersonate French nobility. All the pieces are preceded by explanatory Prologues, often considerably longer than the pieces themselves.

Grammelot: onomatopoeic patter used to imitate foreign languages and exotic dialects.

Fo, *Manuale*, p. 337

There are no references to Mayakovsky — perhaps Fo is merely being coquettish in giving this title to his latest play, in which he is the sole and absolute protagonist. ... The didactic aspect, which uses slides of old woodcuts and etchings, is unable to get rid of vestiges of paternalism, although Fo communicates with his audience with an enormously congenial charge ... rather than the lecture on the conditions of the lower classes, using poetry and medieval theatre, that it undoubtedly is. ... It is a lecture on the theatre: everything that Fo shows and tells us is a representation of the main aspects of a popular theatre which has faded away or been lost in time, and which Fo unearths for us by way of contemporary analogy.

Arturo Lazzari, *L'Unita*, 4 Oct. 1969

Dario began to collate *Mistero Buffo* in about 1963, but he had started doing research on text and the oral tradition even before that. Then he stared translating and re-writing (many of the texts were in Latin or Provençal) adapting them and putting them into theatrical form.

The original idea was to prepare a play making use of the actors in the company, but apart from the difficulties of performing in this abstruse language of the *giullari* ... of the Po valley, we soon realized that these minstrel plays were not designed to be performed in dialogues by more than one actor but as 'racconti' by a single actor, namely the *giullare* himself. ... Gradually Dario worked out the right rhythm and structure through public performances, and began to perform individual pieces, talking about where he had found them, the significance of popular theatre and popular language, and how it had been continually stolen and mystified by the powers-that-be. ... Besides being a play, *Mistero Buffo* is also a living newspaper, continually incorporating current news events and political and cultural satire into performances.

Franca Rame, 1977,
in Tony Mitchell, 'Dario Fo's *Mistero Buffo*', p. 10

Mistero (Mystery) is the term used since the second and third centuries AD to describe a sacred spectacle or performance. Even today in the Mass we hear the priest announce 'In the first glorious mystery ... In the second mystery ...' and so on. So *mistero* means a sacred performance, and *mistero buffo* means a grotesque spectacle.

Fo, *Mistero Buffo*, p. 9

The inventors of the *mistero buffo* were the people. From the first centuries after Christ the people entertained themselves — although it was not merely a from of entertainment — by putting on and performing in spectacles of an ironic and grotesque nature. As far as the people were concerned, the theatre, and particularly the theatre of the grotesque, had always been their chief means of expression and communication, as well as putting across ideas by means of provocation and agitation. The theatre was the people's spoken, dramatized newspaper.

Fo, *Mistero Buffo, p. 9*

The Padano language is reminiscent of Ruzante, but it isn't the language of Ruzante insofar as its concern is to provide an example of an imaginary Esperanto of the poor and disinherited.

Renzo Tian, in Valentini, p. 125

The kind of relationship with his audience that Fo is attempting to establish in *Mistero Buffo* is that between the *giullare* and the peasants. Fo operates continually a double register of medieval satirical, entertaining and abrasive portrayals which are 'buffo' in the jongleuresque sense of the term, and his analogous references to present day reality. As a result he never loses sight of the ultimate aim of the performance ... to raise his audience's consciousness of the repressiveness of the capitalist system. ... His shifts from one register to the other are by no means mechanical, but have a remarkable comic and political alienation effect, which is perhaps the best way of interpreting the success and incisiveness of *Mistero Buffo*.

Mauro Ponzi, *Rinascita*, 28 may 1976, p. 43

... Unilaterally violates fundamental religious values shared by many citizens ... a clear violation of reforms which provided for pluralism, but also mutual respect. ... This programme reminds one of the book-burning of the Nazis, or the fascist attacks on the Vatican newspaper offices and the members of 'Catholic Action'.

Mauro Bubbico
[MP and head of government Media Watch Committee], 1977,
quoted in Fabrizio Carbone, *Proibito in tv*, 1985

I am glad to hear that Fo had an audience of a million and a half, but I'm not sure that all of them were prepared for the violence and aggressiveness of his play. Fo's argument is an elite argument, intended for educated people. Families, and the Italian petit bourgeoisie, are unable to appreciate his argument, and I must insist that TV is a dangerous outlet for this kind of theatre. ... Satire about popes and the bad deeds of the church on earth is as legitimate as any other form of satire, but it's a different matter when it is directed against the gospels.

Franco Zeffirelli, *La Repubblica*, 27 Apr. 1977

Zeffirelli's most serious defect is that he has stifled the festivity, joy and fantasy which exist in all Christian popular tradition and also in the gospels, where there are moments of great festivity and real community. The miracle of the wedding feast of Canaan, for example, the transformation of water into wine, is one of the greatest passages in the gospels, and it's strange that Zeffirelli has censored it. In his film *Jesus* there's no miracle of Canaan, and it's a serious omission, because the

35

audience doesn't get the idea that Christ is also the god of joy and spring, the social and religious continuation of Dionysus. ... His film was a ruling class operation, because he has cut out all the popular content of the gospels.

Fo, *La Repubblica*, 24-25 Apr. 1977

His one man show is the opposite of a personal exhibition. Certainly Fo is here, in his everyday clothes, apparently without any accessories (nothing in his hands, nothing in his pockets, and only a microphone around his neck is visible) on a bare stage, where spectators even sit on the floor. But he is not revealing himself. He is there to perform and show us other people. ... In renouncing any concern with revealing himself and in seeking refuge in characters, Fo is able to compensate for a refusal to be histrionic with another form of histrionics: his virtuosity and his ubiquity. ... Fo is able to play on the timing and the astonishment of metamorphoses. And that is where his commentaries come in. ... In relation to Brechtian epic theatre, Walter Benjamin talks about the 'interrupted act' and the '*gestus* of quotation'. This can be applied here to the letter. Fo engages in continual interruptions. His gestures are abruptly suspended. He observes them, comments on them, laughs at them, repeats them or extends them. ... Through his uncompleted gestures, suspended as it were between past and present, and his words which call up these gestures but are never completely resolved in them, Fo not only appeals to the spectators' imaginations; he activates the spectators. He obliges them to 'accommodate' him continually, to multiply their perspectives and points of view. He engages them in debate.

Bernard Dort, *Théâtre en jeu 1970-1976*,
Editions du Seuil, 1977, p. 207, 208, 210-11

Where English Fo-actors are crude and hysterically over-keen on making you laugh, the original is subtle, at ease with his audience and confident of the intrinsic interest of his material. ... It is great to see someone reviving the traditional enmity between the actor and the church.

James Fenton, *The Sunday Times*, 8 May 1983

All the greater pity, then, that on this occasion Dario Fo has kept to the relatively safe ground of religious satire. In Italy, naturally this reaches into everyone's life. But when we in England (or most of us at least) laugh at the pope, our fun comes easily — we have nothing to lose. ... Italian society has for a sort of shadow, or unconscious structure, all the ceremony, hierarchy and mysticism of the Church. Without this all-pervading ritual it may be that the English will never produce clowns like Fo.

Michael Stewart, 'A Unique Clown', *Tribune*, 6 May 1983

... A revelation comparable to London's first sight of the Berliner Ensemble ...

Irving Wardle, *The Times*, 5 Jan. 1984

If there is a single work that embodies the essence of Fo's epic clown it is *Mistero Buffo*. ... Fo's masterpiece. It provides a key to understanding the extraordinary performance techniques required to animate the texts of his large-cast plays. ... Fo infuses every story with the rhythmic drive of a jazz improvisation, the immediacy of a newspaper headline and the social scope of a historical novel. There is a Marxist slant ... but it is far subtler than the cartoon politics that are often found in commercialized adaptations of Fo's plays in the U.S. Fo's politics are skilfully embedded into the comic structure of his material. Instead of blatantly proclaiming his opposition to economic injustices, Fo creates stories that centre on the tension between freedom and oppression. He then orchestrates his comic climaxes so that they coincide with the victim's liberation from servitude, so that laughter and the defeat of tyranny are simultaneously linked in the audience's mind.

Ron Jenkins, 'Clowns, Politics and Miracles', 1986, p. 13-14

I have studied the camera movements of the cinema, but what I am really trying to recreate is the effects that were employed by medieval painters of the mystery processions. When painters tell a story they are outside language. They don't show the perspective of only one person. They show diverse points of view. In the sacred presentations of the mystery plays in the Middle Ages, people would play a variety of scenes from the life of Christ, showing the actions of Jesus, the Madonna, the devils, etc. And when the painters designed their religious frescoes, they recreated mechanically the things that they had seen from different points of view: the same scene from behind, from the front, from a distance. The techniques of cinema were not born with the invention of the camera. They have been used by painters and storytellers for hundreds of years.

Fo, 1986, in Jenkins, as above, p. 15

The Worker Knows 300 Words, the Boss Knows 1,000 — That's Why He's the Boss

Two-act play.
First production: Teatro della Gioventu, Genoa, 3 Nov. 1969 (dir. Fo).
British production: Yorick Theatre Company, Latchmere Theatre,
    April 1984 (trans. David Hirst; dir. Michael Batz).

A group of workers are clearing out a library in a Communist Party community centre to make way for billiard tables. Some of the books they look through come to life in a series of flashbacks. The first scene deals with the Stalinist trials of the Czechoslovakian activists Kvcanic and Slansky, while the second shows Gramsci as a young student, talking to workers about socialism and persuading them that they must become the intellectuals of the party. In the second act Franca Rame performed the first of her one-woman shows, about the mother of the Sicilian trade unionist Michele Lu Lanzone, who was murdered by the Mafia after discovering a spring in an area of drought. The mother recalls the events from a mental institution. The finale episode deals with Soviet censorship of the poet Mayakovsky's work, his suicide and his mythologizing into a hero. At the end of the play, the workers replace the books and the library, realizing that it is needed.

What does the 300 words mean? It's not our title; it comes from Barbiana, where a group of farm workers wrote a book in which they used this expression ... it means that the boss has built up his own culture, and imposes it on the worker from above, imposing his laws and his vocabulary and way of writing. At home you have a dialect and a culture ... but the boss cuts you off from it. You have 1,000 words of your own culture, but the boss ... insists that you use his, so the 1,000 words refer to the boss's culture ...

    Fo, Debate with an audience, *Compagni senza censura*, 1970, p. 221

... Crude, banal and sentimental, affronting the objectivity of facts by distorting them ...

    Anon., *L'Unita*, 1969, quoted in Valentini, p. 113

Fo ... had an expression of Brecht's in mind: 'The people know how to say profound and complex things with great simplicity; populists who swoop down from above to write for the people say things that are empty and banal, with great simplicity. His ambition was ... to 'make the people speak' and represent on stage problems he had become aware of in his first year, and issues he had heard raised during debates with audiences. His encounter with the world of militants, workers and trade unionists had had a profound effect on him, and stimulated him to express himself in a new way.

Valentini, p. 111

Dario Fo is not only a brilliant satirist: he is also a thinker. He thinks that 'the people' have a vast culture which has almost been obliterated by their oppressors — the church, the state and capitalism. It's the work of his popular theatre to rediscover it. But is there anything to rediscover? *The Worker Knows 300 Words* ... is more about telling the workers what's good for them than about rediscovering.

Desmond Christy, *The Guardian*, 4 April 1985

Chain Me Up and I'll Still Smash Everything

Two one-act plays.
First production: Teatro della Gioventu, Genoa, 5 Nov. 1969 (dir. Fo).
   Law and Order for God and Money's Sake!!!, Capannone
   di via Colletta, Milan, Autumn 1972 (dir. Fo).
British production: The Boss's Funeral, Essex University, 27 Mar. 1987
   (trans. David Hirst; dir. Chris Adamson).
Australian production: The Boss's Funeral University of New South
   Wales, Sydney, 9 Oct. 1984 (trans. and dir. Tony Mitchell).

In The Loom *a communist family who do piece-work at home on weaving looms discover that they have to work sixteen hours a day to meet their overheads. The Mother is staunch in her belief that it is important to follow the precepts of the PCI expressed in their newspaper* L'Unita, *although she never has time to read it, but she becomes aware that the party, in the person of an official who is distributing the piece-work they do, is exploiting them. The father, exhausted by the work and shocked by the fact that his daughter is sleeping with her boyfriend, goes berserk,*

39

smashes the looms, and hits his wife on the head. The Mother, unconscious, dreams about a new, reformed communist party in which revisionists and deviationists have been kicked out. This play was extended into the two-act farce, Law and Order for God and Money's Sake!!! *adding two characters: a prostitute and an extra-parliamentary, revolutionary son.*

In The Boss's Funeral *a group of workers occupying a factory are evicted by the police and decide to stage a play to draw the attention of other workers on their way to work to their predicament. They 'borrow' some costumes and improvise a carnivalesque play about the death of their boss, an unsuccessful attempt at a heart transplant, and the effects of pollution. This develops into a satire about industrial accidents, in which a butcher is brought onstage to slaughter a goat in a bizarre ritual illustrating the need to maintain the daily average of industrial fatalities. This final theatrical device extends into the play's 'third act' : a debate with the audience.*

The characters in the farce ... which the workers perform are the bosses: the boss's widow, the priest, and so on. ... As in Carnival or on New Year's Eve, when you bury the old year. But the worker characters complicate the farce with a device which is intended to give it more impact. ... But the 'sacrifice' would have meant primarily an emotional involvement, which the actors and 'workers' reject. The theatre still serves the function of debating *in front of* an audience and *with* an audience with the tools of farce and satire, and theatrical dialectic, the themes of class struggle, so that everyone ... is a protagonist ...

Fo, in Artese, p. 115, 117

There is nothing more removed from 'agit-prop' in the banal sense of the word, or, on the other hand, from a Pirandellian game in which theatre and reality exhaust each other by reflecting each other. Or rather, it is precisely because Fo's farces use both openly, that they become something else. ... In *The Boss's Funeral* there are three levels interacting: an almost naturalistic account of a factory occupied by its workers surrounded by the police; then the ludic level of the death and burial of the boss enacted by his workers; and the fairy-tale intervention of the Great Vulture 'who transports heavenly souls', also played by a worker. In this detour into fairy tale and cheap romance we recognize the reality of the factory: its smells, pollution, work accidents and exploitation. In the end, the theatre is turned upside down, and reveals its innards. It appears as what it is: the space where a fiction destroys itself in the course of being acted out and extends into the area of class struggle.

Bernard Dort, *Théâtre en jeu*, 1977, p. 204-05

It can't be said that Fo hasn't dealt with current issues in this play. If an Italian theatre exists, it should be produced exactly like this. This is theatre which takes a stand, and uses polemics, both cultural and political, insults, revolt, gripes, falling in love, rational and reckless frenzy, self-observation and observation of others. If there were a hundred plays like (*Law and Order* ...) every year, one could say the Italian theatre was alive. Probably ninety-nine of these plays could be discarded. ... In compensation, however, we would have the delight of feeling that inside the enormous, semi-paralyzed, gaudy but bloodless body of Italian theatre, hot and surging blood had started to flow again. Since there are unfortunately only two or three plays like this a year instead of a hundred, they end up being regarded with suspicion, from the viewpoint of the orderliness and refinement of museum theatre.

Dacia Maraini, *Fare teatro*, 1974, p. 73

... Probably Fo's worst play, *Law and Order* ... was presented (by La Comune) as an example to follow in guilding a class-conscious theatre ...

Valentini, p. 145

The anti-technological and anti-exploitation *topoi* expressed in these two short plays draw their inspiration from the necessity of the moment, that is, by adapting previous works to new situations. ... Studying the differences between the two versions, one can easily explain Fo's militant approach to theatre and particularly the emphasis he places on its didactic and polemical value, over and above its purely aesthetic qualities. In the later version, stress is laid on the message that the only way to bring about any radical social, political and economic change is by building a genuinely revolutionary party. The play is thus not a static presentation of one fixed, immutable message, but a flexible and dynamic instrument of analysis.

Mario B. Mignone, 'Dario Fo — Jester of the Italian Stage', 1981, p. 56

... These one-acts are interesting for their criticism, from a left-wing point of view, of the PCI, which is accused of collusion with the bourgeoisie and reminded of its radical revolutionary duties at exactly the moment when it was widening its power-base towards the centre and evolving the concept of the national path to socialism. What ... emerge ... are Fo's increasingly Maoist views — views not easily tolerated by the PCI.

Lino Pertile, 'Dario Fo', 1984, p. 179-80

I'd Rather Die Tonight If I Didn't Think It Had Been Worth It

'Resistance: the Italian and Palestinian People Speak'

Two-act plays.
First production: Capannone di via Colletta, Milan, 27 Oct. 1970 (dir. Fo).

The titles come from a poem of the Italian Resistance by Renata Vigano, and the play combines readings, songs, mimes and monologues based on accounts of experiences of Italian partisans (in the first act), compared and contrasted with personal testaments by participants in the Palestinian Liberation Movement (in the second act). Put together after only one day's rehearsal, the play was a response to the events of Black September. It includes an account by Franca Rame of Luisa, a woman from Bologna who was tortured and raped by fascists, but who still holds out hopes that communism will come, and an account by Fo of the partisan Angiolino Bertoli who goes on an expedition to blow up an army barracks, and has to hide in a septic tank. In 'The Bestiary', the Russian bear pretends to help the weaker animals of the Middle East against the American tiger, but ends up making an agreement with the tiger and tramples on the rights of the other animals. Another animal fable pits the roosters of Amman against the pigs of King Hussein's police force.

What emerges is a cry of disappointment and revolt rather than a re-evocation; it is an attempt to convey to a present-day audience the revolutionary impulse which inspired the Resistance. ... Fo and Rame reproduce only the more advanced aspects of the Fedayin resistance, those which inspired the overthrow of the old feudal regime before the war against Israel. ... In the second act Fo and his company seek a positive outlet for the disappointments exposed in the first part, talking about a 'people's war'. ... The discussion after the play included among other things not only a violent attack against the USSR, but also an attack against the PCI, which had been presented in the first part as the sole motivating force of the Resistance. ... This really raises the question of who Fo is addressing himself to ... Who does he expect to listen to him?

Edoardo Fadini, *Rinascita*, 13 Nov. 1970

... An extremely effective play; its scrupulous montage was 'scientific', to use Fo's expression ... in the careful precision of the timing, rhythm and tension between performed texts and songs ... and its effectiveness and ability to 'keep the audience nailed to their seats' and lead them into a situation of dialectical conflict and compel them to take up a position ...

Lanfranco Binni, *Attento te!*, 1975, p. 320

Accidental Death of an Anarchist

Two-act play.

First production: Capannone di via Colletta, 10 Dec. 1970 (dir. Fo).

British and Irish productions: Belt and Braces, Dartington College, January, 1979; Half Moon Th., London, Oct. 1979; Wyndham's Th., London, 5 Mar. 1980; TV version, Channel 4, 14 Sept. 1983 (trans. Gillian Hanna; adapt. and dir. Gavin Richards); Oscar Th., Dublin, 10 Feb. 1981 (dir. Jim Sheridan); Contact Th., Manchester, 3 Mar. 1982; Druid Th. Co., Galway, 13 Apr. 1982; Hawks Well Th., Sligo, 10 May 1982; Belltable Th., Limerick, 17 May 1982; Lyric Players Th., Belfast, 18 May 1982; New Vic Studio, Bristol, 18 May 1982; Central Studios, Hampshire, June 1982; Wolsey Th., Ipswich, 24 Nov. 1982; Liverpool Playhouse, 25 Nov. 1982; Cork Th., 26 Jan. 1983; Newcastle Playhouse, 10 Feb. 1983; Chester Gateway Th., 26 Jan. 1983; Theatre Workshop, Edinburgh, 1 Mar. 1983.

American and Canadian productions: Open Circle Th., Toronto, 13 Mar. 1980 (trans. Suzanne Cowan; adapt. and dir. R.G. Davis); Mark Taper Forum, Los Angeles, Jan. 1983 (adapt. John Lahr; dir. Mel Shapiro); Arena Th., Washington, 9 Feb. 1984 and Belasco Th., Broadway, 15 Nov. 1984 (adapt. Richard Nelson; dir. Douglas C. Wager); Eureka Theater, San Francisco, Nov. 1984 (adapt. Joan Holden; dir. Anthony Taccone).

Australian productions: Nimrod Th., Sydney, 11 Feb. 1981, Fortune Th., Canberra, 12 Sept. 1981, and Melbourne Th. Co., 2 Feb. 1983 (trans Tony Mitchell; dir. Brent McGregor); T.N. Th., Brisbane, 29 Feb. 1984 (dir. Rod Wisler).

A 'maniac' infiltrates the Milan Police Station, where an anarchist suspect has 'fallen' to his death from a fourth-floor window during interrogation about a series of bomb explosions in Milan. The Maniac poses as an examining magistrate conducting an enquiry into the anarchist's death, interrogating the police officers who were present at the time of the 'leap'. After demolishing any semblance of credibility in the conflicting and implausible police accounts of events, he convinces them the only solution is to follow the anarchist's example and leap out the window. He then persuades them to construct a new version of events which will win them public sympathy, and which involves singing an anarchist song to prove how well-disposed they were to the suspect. A woman journalist arrives to interview the police for a magazine, and the maniac 'disguises' himself first as a forensic expert, then a bishop, to conceal his 'identity' from her, while managing to convince her the police are responsible for the anarchist's death. Unmasked, the Maniac handcuffs the police, produces a detonator for a bomb which has been shown as evidence, and reveals that he has taped the entire proceedings and will give the tape to the media.

... I realized we needed a decoy character, a surety, so to speak. And then I got the idea that this surety could be a madman who holds the key ... to all the madness, and he becomes normal, while everything else is abnormal. A total reversal. Another important thing we noticed in explanations of the story was indignation ... we realized that indignation is really a means of catharsis, liberation and letting off steam. This ... became central. ... The play was conceived in a grotesque style to avoid any dramatic catharsis. If we had created a dramatic play instead of a comic, grotesque and satirical play, we would have created another liberating catharsis. But this play doesn't allow you this outlet, because when you laugh, the sediment of anger stays inside you, and can't get out. ... It's no wonder dictatorial governments always forbid laughter and satire first, rather than drama.

Fo, 1970, in Meldolesi, p. 178-9

... A grotesque farce about a tragic farce. ... Popular theatre has always used the grotesque and farce — which was invented by the people — to develop dramatic arguments. ... Anger and hatred must become conscious action in collaboration with others, and not just the individual letting off steam in an impotent way. ... This play about the assassination of Pinelli has two main features, which are also pointers towards work and hence confrontation for anyone who is active on the cultural front. First and foremost the 'documentary theatre' aspect; a theatre which sets out to interpret the critical consciousness, which is against any position of flat, naturalistic description of 'phenomena', but has instead a conscious desire for historical and political 'synthesis'. The second feature is that of language which has its roots in the rich cultural heritage of popular culture, satire and grotesque farce.

Fo, Introduction to *Knock, Knock! Who's There? Police!*, 1973, p. 11-13

But what has been the real reason for the show's success? It is not so much the way it mocks the hypocrisies, the lies that are organized so grossly and blatantly (which is putting it mildly) by the constituted organs of the State and by the functionaries who serve them (judges, police chiefs, prefects, undersecretaries and ministers); it has been above all the way it deals with social democracy and its crocodile tears, the indignation which can be relieved by a little burp in the form of scandal; scandal as a liberating catharsis of the system. ... But unluckily for them, they will have to realize that there are a lot of us ... and this time their burp is going to stick in their throats.

Fo, Postscript to *Accidental Death of an Anarchist*,
trans. Ed Emery, 1974, p. 77-8

... An exemplary farce which using the paradoxical techniques of his 'mid-period' plays, dismantles and continually re-assembles, with rapidly mounting pace and entertainment, the false and conflicting versions of the outrageous judicial case presented by the police. This is an example of great theatre, in which the wild inventiveness of the writing blends harmoniously with the aims of counter-information, and succeeds in having a concrete effect on consolidating public opinion in a way one rarely sees happen.

Franco Quadri, 1974, 'Introduction' to *Le commedie di Dario Fo*,
p. xiii-xiv

The most important point about the play is that it is what popular theatre is about, not only in Italy but also in this country. What we haven't really succeeded in doing is adapting a popular form successfully for a larger audience without writing something which either condescends to sexism or racism, or which falls back on the easy jokes, the extremely vicious anti-people edge of humour. Fo is an important lesson for us (in left-wing theatre) because, effortlessly, he destroys the invisible fourth wall and creates live theatre again.

Gavin Richards, *Time Out*, 16-22 Mar. 1979, p. 17

People who refuse to acknowledge that humour and politics are inter-related should keep well away from *Accidental Death of an Anarchist* ... it will only upset them. For everyone else the play will be a delight in terms of both politics and entertainment. ... It is the best that I have seen in this country for the last fifteen years. ... Fo, too close to the bone in Italy, would saw through it in Callaghan's Britain.

Tariq Ali, *Socialist Challenge*, 12 Apr. 1979

... The ultimate in absurdist West End first nights: a mob of be-parka'd, dungaree'd supporters and usherettes touting the *Socialist Worker* and *Socialist Challenge* along with the programmes and ice-creams. With the aid of several excellent players, Gavin Richards, the adaptor, director and lead clown of this essay in Italian agit-prop, turned the auditorium into a fair simulacrum of left-wing pub theatre — with all its good humour and camaraderie, but also with its complacent conviction of being right in being Left.

Victoria Radin, *The Observer*, 9 Mar. 1980

... The danger is that once West End theatre managements have sucked the sugar off Fo's plays, they will quickly spit out the pill. As long as our alternative companies make their main aim transfers to the West End, we are unlikely to see the commitment to mounting Fo for his own sake, in a way that it can reach large audiences.

Lloyd Trott, *The Leveller*, 21 Aug.-3 Sept. 1981, p. 19

I think the image of Italy as seen from abroad is often ridiculous — in the London production of *Anarchist* the characters looked like nine-teenth century Mafioso types, with long sideburns. It was a very glossy production, with stock characters who were like dummies — they reduced the play to a simple farce. Still, it must have been right in terms of the English reality since so many people saw it.

Franca Rame, *Theater*, Summer/Fall 1983, p. 49

Obviously, the shows *have* to be altered when they're transported into a

British context. They take on other values, other modes of expression, other cultural styles, etc. But at the same time, some of the shows — I am thinking of the production of *Accidental Death* ... which I saw here in London — seem to me very overloaded, verging terribly on the grotesque. Many people, though, have said that they liked that production ... even with the excessive buffoonery that they introduced into it. For us this buffoonery is 'anti-style' ... not 'style' in some vague sense, but 'style' in the sense of a satirical form of theatre that seeks to wound, to disturb people, to hit them where it hurts. ... In my opinion these productions lack subtlety. They lack detachment, which must be the first main quality of an 'epic' actor.

Fo, in *Riverside Workshops*, Red Notes, 1983, p. 67-8

The capacity of Fo's buffoon to impersonate policemen, anarchists, judge, and bishop fosters a comic, carnivalesque vision of society where, as Bakhtin said of the carnival in Rabelais's world, people become interchangeable in their mass body. Fo becomes a one-man carnival, and amply represents the collectivity ...

Joel Schechter, 'The Un-American Satire of Dario Fo', 1984, p. 116-17

Don't call my play a comedy. There is a misunderstanding of the word. I call it farce. In current language, farce is understood as vulgar, trivial, facile, very simple. In truth, this is a cliché of official culture. What they call comedy today has lost the rebellious strain of ancient times. What is provocative and rebellious is farce. The establishment goes for comedy, the people for farce.

Fo, Programme Note for Washington Arena Production
of *Accidental Death*, 1984

It didn't work at the Mark Taper Forum ... and ... it doesn't really work on Broadway. But finally an American company has got Dario Fo's *Accidental Death of an Anarchist* right. ... The Eureka Theatre of San Francisco ... had the sense to go to Joan Holden for an adaptation. ... Holden has been writing scripts for the San Francisco Mime Troupe for fifteen years — the closest thing we have to Fo's radical theatre troupe in Italy. Like Fo, Holden knows that the first thing that people's theatre has to do is be entertaining. ... Holden's *Accidental Death* does so, the message snaking in underneath.

Dan Sullivan, *Los Angeles Times*, 25 Nov. 1984

... All the North American productions of *Anarchist*, including my own, have failed to match the author's intentions, have misunderstood the structure of the work, and have not given enough importance to the casting of a recognizably political actor in the lead. ... So far, most U.S. productions of *Anarchist* have tried to downplay or ignore the politics. Producers, directors and players have aimed for a slapstick hit. Their thinking seems to be that the more the play is de-politicized, the better will be its reception from the public and the critics. The rub is that when you ignore the political content of *Anarchist* you swamp both the politics *and* the comedy. It will not serve to cast a clown in the main role. A way must be found to politicize the comedy and fill the politics with humour.

R. G. Davis, 'Seven Anarchists I Have Known', 1986, p. 313, 318

United We Stand! All Together Now! Hang On, Isn't That the Boss?

Two-act play: 'Workers' Struggles, 1911-1922'.
First production: Casa del Popolo, Varese, 27 Mar. 1971 (dir. Fo).

The play follows the political education of Antonia Berazzi, a dressmaker, who develops from an apolitical, ingenuous representative of the world of high fashion into a revolutionary activist. Her husband, Norberto, a militant in the revolutionary wing of the Italian Socialist Party, is killed by a fascist squadron, and Antonia, pretending to be a police informer, infiltrates police headquarters, where a secret deal is taking place involving a trade unionist, an industrialist's wife, a police superintendent, a colonel and a fascist. Antonia avenges her husband by shooting the fascist, and the body is dumped in the same rubbish tip where Norberto was shot along with twenty other comrades. Antonio regrets her action, however, since she has 'killed the dog instead of the masters'. The story proceeds through a series of flashbacks. In 1911, Antonia is caught in a police raid of a subversive meeting at which she is an unwitting participant, and Norberto is arrested after she criticizes Mussolini. Her wedding coincides with Italy's entry into the First World War and clashes between patriots and socialists opposed to the war. In 1917 Antonia visits Norbert in prison, and tells him the Socialist Party leaders have refused to support the insurrectionary struggles in Turin; in 1920 the factory occupations by workers in Turin, led by Gramsci, are shown to be betrayed by the Socialist leaders and trade unionists who make a deal with the government.

Even though the play's predominant form is certainly not grotesque, much of the action which has the dressmaker as its protagonist is made up of farcical gags. Antonia's language is full of proverbs and jargon which have their roots in popular culture. Her character is built around one of the commedia masks: the *étourdie*. She is a kind of vamp who gradually acquires a political conscience and becomes *étourdie* (dim witted) in a cunning and calculating way.

Fo, in *Sipario*, Mar. 1971

While we were touring around the employment centres and co-operative headquarters where the working class invited us for discussions, this historical period kept on coming up — 1911 and the arrival of fascism. A lot of old people who had lived through this period demonstrated in what they said that even they had not become aware of the historical significance of those years. So there was a need for first a clear understanding of them, and then sustained research into them. Since we'd left the bourgeois theatre to put ourselves at the service of the 'working class', we had an obligation to develop this subject, and untangle the confusion, since it involved the origins of the whole workers' movement in Italy. And now that there is a resurgence of fascism it's even more important to understand the origins and reason for today's fascism, even if the situations are different from an objective viewpoint.

Fo, 'Teatro di situazione uguale teatro popolare', *Sipario*,
May 1971, p. 43

... The internal structure is marked by a violent play of emotional chiaroscuro which is sustained by a desire to involve the audience, totally manipulating and controlling them through the mechanism of identification and projection. This is evidenced by the rigid alternation between serious, emotional sequences (which are not tragic, however ...) and comic sequences. ... An often congenial and wildly scatological thread places certain aspects of the play in the equivocal area of provincial vaudeville and popular *avanspettacolo*. Hence it would almost seem that the Gramscian lesson, cited openly here as elsewhere by Fo, of the need for a class culture ... is interpreted in reverse, by retaining from this lesson its ambiguously populist aspects, whereby melodrama and vaudeville are seen as real models for an audience that is more petit bourgeois than working class. For Gramsci, these models were intended to be used in an ... introductory fashion, to initiate a certain type of lively, authentic dialogue with the target audience.

Paolo Puppa, 'L'erba voglia', Apr. 1972

... In the story of the sub-proletarian woman in *All Together Now, United We Stand*, which is about her gaining political awareness, there is a clear historical situation: the disunity of the workers' movement, for which the leaders of the Communist Party are largely responsible on both an ideological and an organizational level. This, together with the split and the lack of faith in the power of the proletariat, are the basis of a real political situation.

The play is about the consciousness of a woman in conflict with her situation of being a woman and being exploited. It even involves a love story, which is not presented in metaphorical terms, but as the living relationship between a woman and a man which is the consequence of this consciousness, and the cultural, political and moral transformation, the ideological and moral change, which is fundamental for this woman.

Fo, 'Some Aspects of Popular Theatre', 1977, p. 133

Fedayin

Two-act play: 'The Palestinian Revolution through its Culture and Songs'.
First production: Capannone di via Colleta, Milan, Jan. 1972 (dir. Fo).

A documentary play about the Palestinian struggles performed by Franca Rame and eight members of the Popular Front for the Liberation of Palestine, with simultaneous translation from Arabic to Italian, slides, masks and songs. A thirteen-year-old girl narrates how she joined the Fedayin at the age of nine, and had to kill another nine-year-old who was wounded, so that she wouln't be captured and interrogated by Hussein's bedouins; in a modern version of the story of Judith and Holofernes, a Palestinian woman sleeps with and then kills a captain from Hussein's police force, a well-known torturer of the Fedayin; a thief gives up his life of crime to join the guerillas; a man fighting on the Al Fatah side sees the error of his ways and joins the Popular Front; women try to prevent ancient traditional customs like their exclusion from funeral services and the whipping of brides on their wedding night; a woman whose Fedayin son has been killed pleads for him not to be made a hero because 'our stories should be true stories about men who trip up, who have constant doubts, who are afraid, but who don't run away'.

... This is not a play conceived along classical lines, nor does it follow any rigidly expository or narrative thread. It is a montage of testimonies, songs, slides, readings from documents, theatre-verité sketches, explanatory speeches and asides, reflections and comments on particular events, more or less along the lines pursued by Piscator in 1925 when he produced *Trotz alleden!* ... Through these means the play achieves more than any work of the imagination could in managing to convey a sense of the upheaval that the Palestinian people have gone through, and gives a desperately epic quality to their struggle for survival. ... The question as to whether or not this is theatre seems an idle one.

Aldo Paladino, *Il Dramma*, Sept.-Oct. 1972, p. 28-30

Apart from the riots and the often pretentious polemics, and despite the later, partly self-critical statement by La Comune and the PFLP that they had dealt too directly with the internal problems of the Palestinian Resistance Movement in a situation of general lack of information (which may have led to sectarian interpretations of the play, particularly its criticisms of the Al Fatah position), *Fedayin* remains a coherently internationalist play, in its production aspects as well as its content ... a militant play in the fullest sense of the word, arising from specific political needs of the [revolutionary] movement in Italy and a concrete response to the need for 'support' on every level, requested by a liberation movement.

Lanfranco Binni, *Attento te!* 1975, p. 338

They were theatrical statements which theatre people made in order not to feel paralyzed by the struggles of particular people. They are useful because they can help others to break out of the same sort of feeling, which is natural because of the alarm which events caused. ... *Fedayin* dealt with the significance of the split between the right and the left of the Palestinian resistance movement, and the crisis in the movement after the massacre in July at Gerashea Ajlun. The limitations of these plays and the information they provide, seen in retrospect, are due to the need for a quick statement, which can lead to presenting arguments which are provisional and hasty.

Fo, in Artese, p. 127-28

Knock, Knock! Who's There? Police!

Two-act play.
First production: Circolo Quarticciolo La Comune, Rome, 7 Dec. 1972 (dir. Fo).

A sequel to Accidental Death of an Anarchist, *performed as a rehearsed reading, and written for the third anniversary of the bomb explosions in Milan's Piazza Fontana, in connection with which the anarchist Pinelli was interrogated. Set in the Italian Ministry of the Interior, with a chorus of civil servants who sing songs commenting on the action, the play begins with investigations into the bomb explosion at the Banca dell'Agricoltura and the police manhunt for the anarchists Valpreda and Pinelli. A taxi driver's evidence suggests that fascists are implicated in the bombing, but the Chief of Secret Police (played by Fo) instructs that fascist leads should not be followed up, despite the known involvement of one Valerio Borghese in an attempted right-wing coup d'état. In the second act, the Prime Minister Andreoti gives orders to direct the police inquiry into right wing terrorist groups. Specific people and events of the 'strategy of tension' are mentioned by name, and continual news updates on events are telephoned in to the Chief. He repeatedly asks what 'the man in the street' thinks about the situation, and attempts to quell the mass movement of mobilization against the 'state massacres' by offering sex and mass executions. The Chief also performs 'Scapino's Grammelot', a lesson in theatrical hypocrisy taken from Molière, which is presented as a demonstration of 'the real art of a Christian Democrat minister'. The play ends with a song inviting people not to 'hang their head, or the boss will break it'.*

... Extends the argument begun in my play about the death of comrade Pinelli. It is a didactic play, and an attempt to synthesize the historical process which is under way: three years of history of the 'state massacres' and their class enemy, the working class and its supporters, who have caused the angry and defensive reaction of the Italian bourgeoisie to action which has been largely spontaneous. In this case the weapon of demystification is again the grotesque. ... The 'state massacres' and their criminal developments have been reconstructed in grotesque form from the point of view of the authorities, in an office which played a fundamental role in the 'Piazza Fontana' operation.

Fo, 'Introduction' to *Knock, Knock!*, 1973, p. 13-14

... Written in seven or eight days, and rehearsed in eight days ... a long gag lasting a good two and a half hours; convulsive and frenetic with telephone calls, functionaries coming and going, orders from the ministry, and the arrival and departure of documents, information, instructions to the police, news, etc. ... In the first act the attacks against the PCI are cautious. In the second act a squalid biliousness emerges, culminating in the final debate, which instead of being a discussion embellishing and correcting the play ... is a tirade indicting our party as the real enemy of the working class.

Edoardo Fadini, *Rinascita*, 22 Dec. 1972

As usual, truncheons speedily interpret the need for law and order. ... The play was not in fact designed to please the police force. ... But Fo and Rame have been making a nuisance of themselves for quite a number of reasons. ... Guaranteeing Fo the freedom to perform does not mean talking about the freedom of art and culture, nor is it the same thing as fighting for Marlon Brando's right to use butter. ... In our permissive society comics have not been a cause of alarm for some time now. But this comic is a cause for alarm, to the extent that there are attempts to get rid of him with police warrants as well as by other means, and to give him a brutal warning: 'If you carry on the way you're going, you're a dead man'. ... Is there any real difference between a country where an MP is beaten up for speaking in parliament and a country where a woman is tortured because she talks about political problems on a stage?

Umberto Eco, 'Pum, Pum! Chi è? Fascisti!', *Espresso*, 18 Mar. 1973

The People's War in Chile

Two-act play.
First production: Palazzo dello Sport, Bolzano, 20 Oct. 1973 (dir. Fo).

A montage of monologues, songs and sketches written and performed by Fo, Rame and the Sicilian 'cantastorie' Cicciu Busacca, in response to the coup in Chile. A duet on the last transmission of the Chilean radio station MIR is followed by a digression on international politics and in particular the Middle East, comparing Golda Meir with a parrot; a song about Murieta, a Chilean activist in the miners' struggle who becomes an outlaw and is killed in a battle, is followed by the Chilean Christian Democratic party, personified as the madam of a brothel, who backs the coup and appeals to the pope for support. An 'incident' occurs in which police messages received in the theatre indicate that there has been a 'coup d'état' in Italy. In the second act, a monologue and songs celebrate the music and revolutionary example of Victor Jara, and 'Cicciu Corno', a piece by Busacca, tells how the donkey used to have a horn with which it defended weaker animals until it was tricked by the powerful animals into cutting it off so they could kill the other animals, proving that only the revolution can save the proletariat. The play ends with 'Mamma Togni', a monologue about a woman who drives away fascist speakers from a platform with a stick, is arrested, but released to general public acclaim, and a discussion with the audience.

...We tried out improvisation techniques; it was a play in which all the actors came on stage one at a time and played characters who were apparently unrelated to one another — it was basically a series of interlinked monologues. But the main element was provocation, which is why we were attacked by some left wing magazines, and by comrades from some groups, for the play's violence and realism in terms of provocation. They said we'd played a 'dirty trick' on them and treated serious matters too lightly, namely the possibility of a coup d'état. ... [In] popular theatre you find the same techniques, namely 'incidents', ruthless violent provocation which makes you sit up straight. ... You find the same sort of provocation in El Teatro Campesino, and again in the stories which comrades tell us now about Margera, where there were demonstrations with Christs on crosses in the streets. ... We realized that our recent experiences had given us the courage to overturn the rules of a theatre which has always been looked upon like the Parthenon.

Fo, 'Popular Culture', p. 53

It is probably the first time in the history of the theatre that an actor was taken directly from the stage to prison, before he had even begun his performance, with an armed escort usually reserved for important criminals.

Chiara Valentini, *Panorama*, 22 Nov. 1973

Can't Pay? Won't Pay!

A farce in two acts.

First production: Palazzina Liberty, Milan, 3 Oct. 1974. New, revised edition, Palazzina Liberty, 16 Sept. 1980.

British and Irish productions: (as *We Can't Pay We Won't Pay!*, trans. Lino Pertile; adapt. Bill Colville and Robert Walker), Half Moon Th., London, 22 May 1978 (dir. Robert Walker); Oxford Th. Group, Edinburgh Festival, Aug. 1980 (dir. Tim Sebel); Overground Th. Company, Kingston, Oct. 1980 (dir. Philip Partridge); Phoenix Arts Th., Leicester, Jan. 1981; Leeds Playhouse, Apr. 1981; (as *Can't Pay? Won't Pay!*) Criterion Th., London, 15 July 1981 (dir. Robert Walker); Victoria Th., Stoke-on-Trent, 6 Oct. 1982; Drumbeat Company, Plymouth, 7 Feb. 1983; Project Arts Centre, Dublin, May 1983; Cambridge Th. Company, May 1983; Legit Th. Company, Dublin, June 1983; Crucible Th., Sheffield, July 1983; Spectacle Th. Company, Glamorgan, Wales, 13 Feb. 1984; Civic Th., Chelmsford, 13 Feb. 1984; Dukes Playhouse, Lancaster, 4 Apr. 1984; Torch Th., Milford Haven, Oct. 1985 (dir. Les Miller).

American and Canadian productions: (as *We Won't Pay We Won't Pay!* adapt. R. G. Davis) Tamahous Th., Vancouver, Sept. 1980 (dir. R.G. Davis); Chelsea Th. Center, New York, 16 Dec. 1980 (dir. R. G. Davis); Empty Space Th., Seattle, 12 May 1981 (dir. Richard Edwards); San Francisco Mime Troupe, 1981 (dir. Joan Holden); (as *We Can't Pay We Won't Pay!*) Open Circle, Toronto, Sept. 1981 (dir. Sylvia Tucker); Los Angeles Actors' Th., Sept. 1981; Wisdom Bridge Th., Chicago, 1985.

Australian productions: (as *We Can't Pay We Won't Pay!* trans. Margaret Kunzle) Wood Street Th., Newcastle, May 1980 (dir. Brent McGregor) ; New Th., Sydney, July 1980; New Th., Melbourne, Apr. 1981; Q Th., Penrith, June 1981; Troupe Th., South Australia, Sept. 1981; Theatre South, Wollongong, Mar. 1982; TN! Th., Brisbane, 24 Mar. 1982; Murray River Performing Group, Dec. 1982 (trans. Lino Pertile; adapt. Bill Colville and

Robert Walker); Universal Th., Melbourne, June 1983
(dir. Lois Ellis); (as *Don't Pay! Don't Pay!* trans. Tony Mitchell)
Theatre ACT, Canberra, 7 Sept. 1985 (dir. John Derum).

Antonia, a working-class Milanese woman, has pilfered some goods from her local supermarket after a protest against rising prices has developed into a riot of looting. She and her neighbour Margherita set about trying to hide the stolen goods from their line-toeing PCI husbands, and Margherita stuffs a bag of groceries down her coat. Giovanni, Antonia's husband, catches sight of Margherita on his arrival home, and Antonia tells him Margherita is pregnant but has been hiding the fact. Antonia goes to Margherita's place to borrow something for dinner, and Giovanni is visited by a Maoist police constable who is searching their apartment block for stolen goods, but is in favour of civil disobedience. Antonia returns with Margherita, and they are searched again by more police, who end up taking both women to a maternity hospital for a 'baby transplant'. Luigi, Margherita's husband, arrives with news that he, Giovanni and their work-mates have been made redundant. Giovanni tells him of his wife's 'pregnancy', and they set off for the maternity hospital. In Act Two, Antonia and Margherita, after giving police and hospital the slip, return home and start transporting the shopping to a garden shed. Luigi and Giovanni meet the Maoist constable again at a road accident involving a truckload of stolen sacks of sugar, rice and flour. Encouraged by the constable, they steal some sacks and transport them home in a coffin. A police sergeant apprehends the two women with their 'pregnant' bellies, but they convince him he has gone blind when the electricity is cut off, and blow up his stomach with oxygen in an attempt to revive him when he knocks himself unconscious. Finally, the thefts by both the husbands and the wives are revealed to one another, Giovanni is convinced that civil disobedience is the only effective way of fighting oppression and exploitation, the police sergeant revives, convinced he is pregnant, and in a riot in the street hundreds of women drive away a battalion of police.

As in the old (or ancient would be more appropriate) Neapolitan and

56

Venetian popular farces, the starting point, the fundamental impetus, is hunger. The initial, instinctive solution in which everyone takes care of themselves in resolving the atavistic problem of appetite develops into a need to work collectively, to get organized and fight together — not just for survival, but to live in a world where there are less brightly-lit shop windows, less motorways, and no government corruption, no thieves — the real thieves, the big fish, that is — and where there is justice, justice for all! …

We've tried to avoid the pitfalls of ideological didacticism by means of a 'theatre of situation'. This is a means similar to that of 'epic theatre', where it's not the characters who advance the action, but the situation, the theatrical mechanism.

The development is determined and sustained by events, and the characters involved in the situation are the gears which move or manoeuvre this mechanism. This flick of a switch can release a mechanism of paradox, then blow it up like a photo, intensify it, stand it on its head, speed it up, or explode it.

This isn't a choice of 'career', even if the career aspect of this type of theatre is important. It's a cultural choice, because being involved in a theatre of situation means representing a story rather than acting it. It means not being involved in the 'drama' arising from the individual character and his or her private and individual problems and relationships with others, but rather dealing with everybody's problems in the context of a collective drama. These problems emerge in an explosive way in a dialectical conflict of relationships within a 'situation' …

The actual draft of the play is my sole responsibility, but from the first improvised reading to the final mise en scène the text has been discussed repeatedly, not only among our collective, but above all with workers' groups and committees from various different factories in Milan. This is, in our opinion, the correct way to run a 'collective' theatre.

Fo, 1974, 'Editorial Note' to *Non si paga! Non si paga!*, 1974

Deals with the very vital current issue of civil disobedience, in the form of battles against increases in market and service prices, new instances of which are continually being reported in the newspapers. But what is outstanding about it is that Fo, with the sensibility and awareness that make him one of the most extraordinary figures in Italian theatre, has imagined these episodes before they actually happened. Then reality began to imitate art.

Alberto Blandi, *La Stampa*, 3 Oct. 1974

Mass illegality, *autoriduzione* and the like are not only all over and done with, but forgotten issues after years of bloodshed. Ideas like socialism and revolution and the working class have become much more complex (not to mention confused), and seeking an impetus for action has now become somewhat difficult. ... Amidst the laughter at the implausible twists and turns of this extremely threadbare story, or one of Fo's gags, which are getting more and more re-cycled and almost as if quoted from his arsenal in a process of self-codification like Eduardo [De Filippo], amidst the *lazzi* and the games, embarrassment and annoyance crept in ... [and] a discomfort not at the politics, but at the rhetoric of the politics.

Ugo Volli, *La Repubblica*,
19 Sept. 1980

The motivations for putting on these plays are different from ours. When we did *Non si paga! Non si paga!* we started from a real situation, just as the work we did on women was very precise, both theatrically and ideologically. [In London] *Non si paga!* is taken just as a play, without any real starting point. In my show, because I've worked on it, and especially because I've worked on it with audiences, I get a thousand or so laughs. Here it's a couple of hundred, because they've cut the translation, chucked out what they don't understand, and distorted the overtly political aspects.

Franca Rame, *Sipario*,
Sept. 1983, p. 37

The grotesquery of the situations in which Fo's characters find themselves is almost Rabelaisian. Bakhtin noted that in Rabelais's world, the grotesque 'discloses the potentiality of an entirely different world, of another way of life ... a return to Saturn's golden age ... [requiring] bodily participation in the potentiality of another world.' ... A police officer appears to experience an hysterical pregnancy ... several women stuff boxes of pasta and vegetables under their coats, so that they look pregnant; their husbands almost instantly accept the roles of worried, expectant fathers. ... The resulting farce offers a vision of urban Saturnalia, where instead of Rabelaisian monks, pilgrims, or scholars, we see housewives, factory workers, and police officers undergo illegal or bizarre transformations in body, and in their relations to nature (vegetables, birth) and private property (unaffordable groceries). ... Rabelais's grotesquery has given way to antic transformations more suitable for an age of inflation, shoplifting, and miracle salad dressing.

Joel Schechter, 'The Un-American Satire of Dario Fo',
1984, p. 117-18

Fanfani Kidnapped

A play in three acts and two interludes.
First production: Palazzina Liberty, Milan, 5 June 1975 (dir. Fo).

A bitterly hilarious indictment of the Christian Democratic Party (DC), personified by one of its most important leaders: former Italian Prime Minister and one-time DC secretary, Amintore Fanfani. The action begins with a political kidnapping: Fanfani is abducted on the orders of none other than the Christian Democratic Prime Minister Giulio Andreotti, for the purpose of arousing a wave of public outrage and sympathy calculated to win votes for the DC in the forthcoming elections (the first performance of the play was held on 5 June 1975, just ten days before nationwide regional elections). Believing himself in the hands of an authentic terrorist group, Fanfani blurts out a hysterical 'confession' in which he admits to all the corruption, clericalism, repression and unscrupulous opportunism which have marked the party's thirty-year-old administration. At a certain point, faced with the impending discovery of their hideout, the kidnappers are obliged to move Fanfani to a new location: a private, very exclusive abortion clinic directed by nuns. They disguise him as a woman and, terrified by the prospect of mutilation or death, he is assailed by a violent attack of intestinal gas, which swells his stomach to pre-delivery proportions. In order to avoid a veritable explosion, he must undergo a caesarean section. When his stomach is cut open, releasing a violent stream of gas and smoke, Fanfani gives birth to a remarkable infant: a fascist puppet decked out in fez and black shirt. During the grotesque delivery, Fanfani dies and is immediately transported to heaven, where Jesus, Mary and St. Michael — represented as militant leaders and defenders of the poor — are waiting to sit in judgment on him. During the 'trial', the most scathing indictment of Fanfani's crimes comes from the Virgin, who condemns him and his party to perdition. Before being banished from heaven, however, he is forced to listen to Mary's prediction of the future. In a madly surrealistic climax, a sort of witches' sabbath in heaven, she foretells the eventual disaster which awaits the Christian Democrats and the ultimate triumph of the revolutionary working class. At this point Fanfani wakes up in his office to discover that the entire episode has been a dream. However, in one of Fo's most clamorous surprise endings, the dream proves to be real after all: no sooner does he come to his senses than a group of kidnappers — flesh-and-blood ones this time — breaks into his office, informs him that the abduction has ben arranged by Andreotti, and drags him, screaming, away.

> Suzanne Cowan, 'Dario Fo: Bibliogaphy, Biography, Playography',
> 1978, p. 20

[It] is not a cabaret, nor is it a satire of a famous member of the government and his mannerisms and weaknesses. It is a grotesque representation of authority, and the excessive arrogance of Christian democratic power. In other words, the play doesn't set out to show that Fanfani is a villain and the DC is his victim. It explains that Christian Democracy as a whole has represented a moral outrage for thirty years in its arrogance, its contempt for the people, and its embezzlements.

> Fo, in *Panorama*, 12 June 1975

A complicated ... fable which is unchecked by any artistic restraint, freewheeling in a ramshackle and haphazard way with a crudeness that lashes out at any target; sometimes the Communist Party, sometimes, obviously, the Christian Democrats — frontally and indiscriminately. ... Once again the extremist parameters of Fo's vision, combined with his demagogy, take him a long way outside the concrete reality of political struggles in Italy. When all is said and done, his *Fanfani Kidnapped* is an innocuous bogey.

> Arturo Lazzari, *L'Unita*, 7 June 1975

Mother's Marijuana Is the Best

A two-act play.
First production: Palazzina Liberty, Milan, 2 Mar. 1976.

In a working class family, mother (Rosetta, Franca Rame) and grandfather (Fo) use various types of drugs, from 'grass' to scorpion punctures (sic), also growing their own and dealing on a small scale among their neighbours. After a series of argu-

ments with their son/grandson Luigi and his friend, who is on 'hard' drugs, the by-now experienced drug-takers unmask a priest, who is an informer and member of the Mafia, and throw him out of the window together with a policeman from the narcotics squad. ... The defenestration is the culmination of a series of ritual punishments to these symbols of authority, carried out in order to damage their dignity and physical well-being: their trousers are pulled down and their bottoms branded, and there is an account of the injuries Rosetta inflicts on the carabiniere Antonio. The couple finally reveal to the youngsters that their addiction has been faked, as a strategy to teach both of them a lesson. Ordinary cigarette smoke and plastic scorpions have been used to demonstrate the class and ideological function of drugs, which divert, mystify and dissipate authentic class struggle.

Cappa and Nepoli, p. 116-17

We do not tell stories from the past ... we are exclusively interested in what is happening now. We deal with drugs that are still distributed under the name of psycho-pharmeceuticals to make workers work harder, and we attempt to make young people understand, and to understand better ourselves, all the pitfalls which the authorities, and not only the authorities, have surrounded this problem with. ...

We have attempted to be as informative as possible ... without providing any definitive solutions. And above all we have tried to involve people by entertaining them, making them laugh until they get gooseflesh, if possible. We think that the intelligence that operates through satire and mockery, along with the rationality of irony, is, when all's said and done, the best and healthiest of drugs, particularly when obtuse authorities are trying to repress every citizen who has any ideas about freedom.

Fo, 'The Invention of Drugs',
La marijuana della mamma è la più bella, 1976, p. 23

The initial impetus is excellent, and some of the gags (like the grandfather's surreal monologue and LSD trip) ... are of a high standard. Less plausible from a theatrical point of view is the series of strictly didactic speeches, where the counter-information aspects break the farcical structure. ... But when the antidote of satire restores the balance of this thesis play and reaches the extremes of lunacy that are a trademark of Fo's plays, the play displays an inventiveness and comic force.

Cappa and Nepoli, p. 117

61

Female Parts
(All House, Bed and Church)

By Franca Rame and Dario Fo.

First production: Palazzina Liberty, Milan, 6 Dec. 1977.
Second Edition, Teatro Cristallo, Milan, 27 Feb. 1981 (dir. Fo).
Performed by Rame (as *It's All Bed, Board and Church*) at Riverside
Studios, London, 11 May 1982 and in Apr. 1983, at the Edinburgh
Festival in Aug. 1983, and on tour in the USA in 1986, beginning at
the American Repertory Th., Cambridge, Mass., May 1986.

British and Irish productions: (trans. Margaret Kunzle;
adapt. Olwen Wymark; dir. Michael Bogdanov; with
Yvonne Bryceland) National Th., London, 26 June 1981.
Glasgow Th., Scotland, Aug. 1982; Borderline Th. Company, Irvine,
Scotland, Jan. 1983; Project Arts Centre, Dublin, 17 Feb. 1983;
Northern Lights Th., Yorkshire, June 1983; Worcester Repertory
Company, 13 Feb. 1984; Contact Th., Manchester, June 1987
(dir. Sheryl Crown); (Second Edition, as *The Fourth Wall*,
trans. Gillian Hanna; dir. Penny Cherns; with Paola Dionisotti)
Monstrous Regiment, the Drill Hall, London, Mar. 1983.

American and Canadian productions: Pepsco Summer Fair, Novoton,
USA, 21 July 1982; New Stagecraft Company, New York,
4 Nov. 1982; New Rose Th., Portland, Oregon, 3 Mar. 1983;
H.T. Studios, Toronto, Mar. 1983; Empty Space Th., Seattle, Spring,
1984; Los Angeles Actors' Th., 1984; (First and Second Editions, as
Orgasmo Adulto Escaped from the Zoo, adapt., dir., and performed by
Estelle Parsons) Public Th., New York, 27 July. 1983.

Australian productions: Nimrod Th., Sydney, 10 Feb. 1982
(dir. Fay Mokotow); T.N! Th., Brisbane, 24 Mar. 1982; Winter Th.,
Fremantle, 4 June 1982; Theatre ACT, Canberra, 8 Oct. 1983
(dir. Anne Harvey); Universal Th., Melbourne, Feb. 1984
(dir. Lois Ellis; with Evelyn Krape); (Second Edition, as *Whore in a
Madhouse*, trans. Gillian Hanna) Belvoir St. Th., 11 Apr. 1985.

---

*A series of monologues dealing with female oppression. In
'Waking Up', a working class woman goes through her morning
chores preparing for work and to take her baby to nursery, but
cannot find her key. In order to work out where she has left it,
she retraces everything she has done since arriving home the
night before, including a prolonged argument with her husband
— who sleeps throughout the play — about the injustice of her*

situation. Having found the key, she realizes that it is Sunday. In 'A Woman Alone', an attractive housewife is locked in the house by her suspicious husband, whose brother, confined to a wheelchair, gropes at her periodically, while a peeping-tom spies on her from the building opposite. She recounts her life story to a neighbour, telling her of a sexual escapade with her English teacher, who appears and harasses her, followed by one of her husband's creditors. At the end of the play, she takes a gun and shoots all the men who are oppressing her. In 'The Same Old Story', a woman falls pregnant to her left-wing, intellectual lover, whom she cannot persuade to be considerate of her. In a prolonged, scatological children's story, she tells about a little girl with a dolly who uses swearwords, and influences her to marry a engineer who exploits her as a sex object. After the engineer tries to kill the doll, she blows him up until he explodes, and ends up under a tree with a group of other girls who all have 'the same old story'. In 'Freak Mother', a woman becomes a hippy in order to pursue her son, who has joined a commune of 'Metropolitan Indians'. After experimenting with promiscuity, becoming a witch, and resorting to crime, she hides in a church, where she recounts her story to a priest in confession. Then there is a Medea based on the popular shows of the magicians of Umbria and Tuscany, a Medea who does not kill her own children out of anger and jealousy, but out of her awareness that the children are the links of a chain that society hangs around the neck of women 'like a heavy wooden saddle that makes us easier to milk and easier to mount'. The Second Edition added a 'Prologue' developing an extended word-play on the names of male and female sex organs, 'Contrast for a Single Voice', in which a woman gains the upper hand in seducing her silent suitor by tricking him into believing her parents are sleeping in the next room and he must be extremely furtive, and a 'Roman Lysistrata' recounting a brief version of Aristophanes' play in Roman dialect, which was later discarded. Other monologues Rame performed sporadically included 'Monologue of a Whore in a Madhouse', in which a prostitute tells her life story to a psychiatrist interviewing her in a mental institution, 'Alice in Wonderlessland', in which Carroll's Alice is cast adrift in a porno-world of sexual harassment run by a porno film director (a monkey who is a friend of the white rabbit, and ends up being produced on a conveyor belt as a compendium woman), and 'Michele Lu Lanzone', a monologue taken from The Worker Knows 300 Words.

... For a theatre like ours, which follows hard on current events and is at the same time shaped by them, it would have been a very grave oversight to have failed to have picked up on the women's question. The feminist problem is far too important now. These girls, or rather women, have done some extraordinary things, while, like any movement, they also have their negative and mistaken aspects. But this happens in all real movements. ... I have a lot of esteem for the feminists, especially those who are not completely antagonistic towards men, and those who are working courageously to change things, working in local communities, and with abortion, etc. I am not a militant feminist, since most of my time is taken up with theatre, 'Red Aid', and a thousand and one other things that have to be done to keep things afloat. But I do follow the developments and activities of the feminist movement.

Franca Rame, in *Il teatro politico di Dario Fo*, 1977, p. 144-5

I would never have been able to write female characters that were substantial enough, and — without being modest about it — which have a certain weight, if it hadn't been for Franca. She is a formidable critic and has an extremely good theatrical ear. This is not by chance, but because of the fact that she was born on the stage, almost in the literal sense of the term, and as a result breathed the air of performance before she was even aware of it. Franca's input, not only in drafting characters that involved her directly, but in the overall construction of the comic-grotesque-satirical situation of the plays, has always been a theatrical source for me.

Fo, in *Il teatro politico di Dario Fo*, p. 149-50

... Not a play, or a drama or even a farce. They are bits and pieces of reality that fly through the air and land on us, eliciting wry smiles and uncomfortable admissions.

S. Borelli, *L'Unita*, 11 Dec. 1977

I've understood completely what the condition of women and wives involves, especially that of the wife of a famous actor like Fo. It means always being put in second place in relation to a man, and being judged as incapable of any autonomous choice.

Rame, in *Panorama*, 20 Dec. 1977

... High grade feminist farce. ... This, of course, is against the English tradition. We tend to put serious business into straight plays and reserve popular forms, like panto, farce and sitcom, for trivia.

Michael Billington, *The Guardian*, 28 June 1981

The English actress was very good and the direction was very accurate. However, it got a lot fewer laughs than it did in Italy, and less applause. This I think is because it was a different type of theatre from ours — it was a more naturalistic type of acting and direction. We always try to eliminate the superstructure, the excess, because the most important thing is the content. This is a theatrical choice which is epic rather than naturalistic.

Rame in conversation with Tony Mitchell, May 1982

The pieces are comic, grotesque, on purpose. First of all because we women have been crying for two thousand years. So let's laugh now, even at ourselves. And also because a certain gentleman of the theatre, who knew a lot, a certain Molière, used to say: When you go to the theatre and see a tragedy, you identify, empathize, cry, cry, cry, then go home and say, 'What a good cry I had tonight,' and you have a good night's sleep. The social significance went by like water over glass. But for us to provoke you to laughter — and it's always Molière who speaks — you have to have a brain, you have to be alert ... to laugh you throw open your mouth and also your brain and into your brain are hammered the nails of reason. We hope tonight that someone will go home with his or her head nailed down.

Rame, 'Prologue', 1981, adapt. Estelle Parsons, *Orasmo Adulto*, p. 4

What most immediately strikes one about Franca Rame is that she is sexy. But rather than serving to undermine the message of her plays, as her detractors allege, it is this very sexiness which gains her access to the women that adamantly feminist theatre will never reach. ... Rame's alternately coy, bawdy and careless sensuality invites women who still aspire to Physical Glamour and the Institution of the Family to relate to and sympathize with characters very much like themselves, while the poignant ironies of the situations enacted gently prod them to broach the issue of their own exploitation. ... Hers is a 'popular' approach to feminism, a blend of mime, story-telling, burlesque and stand-up comedy — all traditions rooted in popular theatre — which can be appreciated by the masses, not just the converted.

Barbara Schulman, 'It's All Bed, Board and Church',
Plays and Players, July 1982, p. 33

There is a quarter of an hour of great theatre in … Franca Rame's new show … the monologue of 'The Rape'. Few know it, only her close friends, but the actress is playing herself: she transposes an appalling experience which actually happened a few years ago (a kidnapping and rape by a group of fascists in the darkness of a van) into pure theatrical expressiveness. Beyond the moral and political impetus which has propelled this fiercely committed performer for years on the civil rights front, the gamble of 'replaying oneself' on stage is an enormous challenge. Rame meets it completely, insofar as she manages to overcome any naturalistic identification, while still conveying all the horror of the degradation she underwent.

Guido Davico Bonino, *La Stampa*, 18 Feb. 1984

Her theatre does not explore relationships among women, and it avoids the mother-daughter relationship so dear to the avant-garde of the feminist movement. If her feminism is elemental, and focuses on the issues of power in heterosexual relationships, it also goes beyond idiosyncratic anti-male positions. The plays suggest that the dynamics of power and liberty, violence and love, conventionality and authenticity, is what really is at stake in women's issues.

Anderlini, p. 39

Tale of a Tiger and Other Stories

A 'giullarata'.
First production: Palazzina Liberty, 2 Feb. 1978 (dir. Fo). Annotated version included in TV programme 'Tricks of the Trade', RAI 3, Mar. 1985.
First British performance: of 'Tale of a Tiger', by Chris Adamson, Essex Univ., 25 Mar. 1987 (trans. Ed Emery; dir. Chris Adamson).
First Australian performance: of 'Tale of a Tiger', Zootango Th., Tasmania, Oct. 1987 (trans. Ed Emery; perf. Ian Laing).

His Story of the Tiger *comes from a Chinese piece which Fo says he saw delivered by a peasant storyteller to an audience of 20,000 when he visited the Chinese People's Republic in 1975. … The 'tiger story' is a fable about a Chinese soldier of Mao's army who returns from the war of liberation. He is wounded and takes refuge in a cave where he is taken care of by a tigress. He gets better and becomes a friend of the tiger family which he takes with him back to his village. The tigers become inseparable friends of the people and help them to rout the last members of Chiang-Kai-shek's army. The 'People's Government' then takes over and doesn't approve of the tigers. An official wants them to be sent to the zoo. The 'people' now have a democratic government so shouldn't need 'tigers' to protect them. In the end, however, the villagers set the tigers against their new leaders.*

John Francis Lane, International Daily News, 1 Apr. 1980

In 'The First Miracle of the Infant Jesus', an 'apocryphal' gospel story, Christ and the Virgin Mary are Palestinian migrants in Egypt. Jesus is ostracized by the other children because he is Palestinian, until he starts creating real birds out of paper ones. The jealous son of the city's biggest landowners destroys the children's games, so Jesus, with permission from his father in heaven, performs a miracle on him. His eyes emit lightning bolts and the boy turns into a terracotta pot. Mary persuades Jesus to change him back, as she and Joseph have managed to find work and do not want to have to be on the run again. Jesus does so, but gives the boy a kick in the bum in the process. 'The Sacrifice of Isaac' is the result of a bet between God and the Devil about the extent of Abraham's love for God. This is revealed to Isaac only after the Angel has appeared to stop Abraham from carrying out the sacrifice of his son. Isaac throws a stone which hits Abraham on the head, and tells his father the stone has fallen from heaven. 'Daedalus and Icarus' begins with the father and son getting lost in the labyrinth they have constructed for Gnossus, and ends with the fall of Icarus after their attempts to fly. Fo uses the story to attack patriarchal power and stress the importance of the imagination, as opposed to surrogate substitutes for the imagination like drugs, horoscopes and UFOs.

In China the tiger has a very precise allegorical significance: they say that a woman, or a man, or a people, have the tiger when they are confronted by enormous difficulties, and at the point where most people are inclined to flee, scarper, run away and abandon the struggle, piss off and even reach the point of denigrating themselves and everything generous they've done before, they insist on standing firm and resisting. ... Another clear allegorical meaning the tiger has, which is perhaps fundamental, is this: a person has the tiger when he never delegates anything to anybody, and never tries to get other people to resolve his own problems. ... The person who has 'the tiger' gets directly involved in the situation, participating in it, controlling it, verifying it, and being on the spot and responsible right up to the end.

Fo, *La Storia della tigre*, 1980, p. 8-9

The *discorsi*, analyses and polemics have their own separate place in the spectacle, introducing and motivating the individual pieces Fo performs or relates. The structure ... takes the form of a text, an explanation, and another text. The fact that the explanations are as entertaining and as well received as the pieces in the play doesn't change the situation. The opposition between language and dialects, between direct dialogue with the audience and fictional story-telling to an ideal audience, between mime and the display of vocal resources, distinguishes perfectly the two areas of the spectacle, which are integrated and complementary, both bringing laughter and applause

Ugo Volli, *La Repubblica*, 3 Mar. 1979

... I performed ['Tale of a Tiger'] in public for a good two years using only improvisation, and I only decided to write it down fairly recently. ... The first performance of this 'giullarata' took place in Florence several years ago ... I decided to try a new piece. I had made a rough draft of the story, but it wasn't written down, the sequence of various passages was in my head ... and then I took off! ... No one, not even Franca, knew I was going to try it out. It was a surprise for the whole company. The performance lasted exactly twenty-five minutes. It was an immediate success. ... But I'd made mental notes that a lot of the elaborations didn't quite work yet, and there were useless repetitions ... passages that were underdeveloped, or too descriptive ... and a lot of approximation. The next day I listened to the tape (of my performance). ... Ten days later, after more cutting, editing and compressing, finally 'The Tiger' lasted fifty-five minutes. It might seem paradoxical, but it's true. In the theatre, often when you cut words the playing time expands because pauses, laughter, and the enjoyment of the actor and the audience come into play.

Fo, *Manuale minimo*, p. 215-16

Trumpets and Raspberries

Two-act play.
First production: Cinema-Teatro Cristallo, Milan, 14 Jan. 1981 (dir. Fo).
British productions: (as *Hooters, Trumpets and Raspberries,*
    trans. R. C. McAvoy and Anna-Maria Gingni) reading at Riverside
    Studios, London, 3 Jan. 1984 (dir. George Byatt); (as *Trumpets and
    Raspberries*) Palace Th., Watford, 4 Oct. 1984, and Phoenix Th.,
    London, 15 Nov. 1984 (dir. Roger Smith); Borderline Th., Murray
    House Th., Edinburgh, Aug. 1985 (dir. Morag Fullerton).
American productions: (as *About Face,* trans. Dale McAdoo and
    Charles Mann; dir. Andrei Belgrader), Yale Rep. Th., New Haven,
    8 Apr. 1983; Eureka Theatre, San Francisco, Aug. 1986; Tomi Park
    Royale Th., New York, 11 Nov. 1987 (dir. Richard Seyd).
Australian productions: (trans. McAvoy-Giugni) Melbourne Th.
    Company (dir. John Sumner), 8 Nov. 1985; T.N! Th., Brisbane,
    June 1986; Th. South, Woolongong, June 1986 and Seymour Centre,
    Sydney, Jan. 1987 (dir. Des Davis); West Australian Th. Company,
    Perth, Sept. 1986 (dir. Simon Phillips); (trans. Tony Mitchell;
    adapt. Greg McCart) New Moon Th., Queensland, 18 Sept. 1985
    (dir. Helmut Bakaitis); Tau Th., Canberra, 16 June 1987
    (dir. Tina Van Raay); State Th. Company, Darwin, June 1987
    (dir. Aubrey Mellor).

---

*Antonio Berardi, a Fiat worker, unwittingly rescues Fiat boss
Gianni Agnelli from a car accident following a botched attempt
by terrorists to kidnap him. Agnelli's face is disfigured in the
crash, and after Antonio flees, leaving his jacket over Agnelli,
the latter is mistaken for Antonio and undergoes plastic surgery
giving him Antonio's face. Antonio's wife Rosa takes Agnelli
home from hospital, believing him to be her husband (the real
Antonio has been living with his mistress, Lucia). Antonio goes
into hiding for fear he will be implicated in the terrorist
kidnapping, but police suspicions are instead directed at
Agnelli. In the ensuing confusion of identities, Rosa believes
they are one and the same person and Agnelli persuades her to
hide him. The house is invaded by rival factions of the Italian
secret police in a series of disguises, and Agnelli reveals he has
plagiarized Aldo Moro's letters to the government, requesting an
exchange of political prisoners for his safety. The request is*

69

successful, proving that wealthy industrialists have more political weight than prominent politicians.

At the end of one of the first performances … three women, relatives of prisoners from Trani, got up on stage and asked if they could read a document. The document … was simply a complaint which they … had sent to the magistrate in that city. … In the eyes of the three journalists who reported the evening, ten people out of the seven hundred plus who packed the theatre were transformed into a tidal wave, a chorus of indignant revolt. The document, which was published in [a number of left-wing Italian newspapers] was transformed into a bulletin for the Red Brigades, even a proclamation calling for a general revolt.

> Fo, 'Newspaper Terrorism', in *Clacson, trombette e pernacchi*,
> 1981, p. 101

Even with Agnelli's final paean to economic power, in New Haven the play hardly offers the universal affront that it poses in Milan. … Moreover, Fo's political critique is more complex and sophisticated than an American audience may be used to, especially in the theatre, for Fo not only jabs the bourgeoisie and the powerful, or simply pits left against right. He also criticizes the left from the left and presents various viewpoints within a broad political spectrum, none of which fare too well under his scrutiny. This complexity is difficult to transfer to America where the left is often perceived and referred to as a single, unified, Soviet-inspired position. But instead of undertaking the difficult task of finding a way to translate the play into a version that could explore these issues for an American audience, the Yale Rep production remains in safely distant Italy.

> Alisa Solomon, *Performing Arts Journal*, No. 20, 1983, p. 65

Fo remains consistent in a theatrical form which speaks the language of politics and ideology to the point of verbose preaching and to the limits of a public debate, and defends his exclusive speciality, the ever-more indiscriminate and mechanical entertainment of an audience which has reached very high figures at his plays. The theatrical quality has declined, and instead of a unified inventiveness and a consistently sustained central idea there is a rigid, schematic application of infantile or simplistic pedagogical and political conceptions.

> Sergio Colomba, *La scena del dispiacere*,
> Ravenna/Longo, 1984, p. 189

… Much of the piece consists of basic slapstick. All the stronger are the moments when Fo clenches his fist and tops the straightforward clown routines with tremendous political gags. ... As in his previous work, there is a seamless connection between the clown and the ideologue; and the bigger the jokes the more intransigent the intelligence behind them.

Irving Wardle, *The Times*, 5 Jan. 1984

The Obscene Fable

Four monologues.
First performance: Cinema Smeraldo, Milan, 11 Mar. 1982 (dir. Fo).
First British production: Young Vic., London, 31 Mar. 1987
  (trans. Justin Gregson; dir. Michael Batz).

His first tale concerns the revolt of a large band of Bolognese citizens in 1324. The revolt is not prominently featured in history books, for reasons that become apparent as the story unfolds. After they suffered huge losses in misguided religious wars, angry Bolognese citizens rebelled against papal legates and the Provençal troops protecting the Vatican's emissaries. The papal delegation, well-supplied with food and whores inside a fortress, found itself besieged by a people's army that used the only weapon available to it at the time: its own excrement. After eleven days, during which the excrement was constantly thrown over the fortress walls, the refined papal sensibilities could take no more. The Provençal troupes and legates left the region under a shower of human ordure.

Joel Schechter, 'Dario Fo's Obscene Fables', p. 88

'The Bologna Riot' is followed by 'The Butterfly Mouse', a twelfth-century sexual fable about a wealthy but simple-minded goatherd who is tricked on his wedding night by his wife, who has been married off to him to avoid the scandal arising from her affair with the local parish priest. When her new husband finally returns from a wild goose chase, she, tired from frolicking with the priest, tells him she has left her sex (the 'butterfly mouse') at her mother's house. The goatherd goes there and is given a cardboard box with a cloth and a mouse in it, and told not to open it until he gets back to his wife. But he

71

*opens it and the 'sex' escapes. When he returns empty-handed
and exhausted to his wife, she takes pity on him and shows him
where the 'butterfly mouse' really is. 'Lucio and the Donkey' is
loosely based on Apuleis'* The Golden Ass. *A poet suffering
from 'phallocratophantasmagoria' tries to transform himself
into an eagle, but ends up as a donkey, who is then forced to
carry the beautiful daughter of a wealthy family. He is
constantly kicked in the testicles by all and sundry, but manages
to rescue the girl from brigands and return her to her parents,
who try to gratify his insatiable sexual appetite with horses.
They then discover he can write, and sell him to a circus, where
he is rented out to an aristocratic lady for sexual purposes, and
he takes part in a live sex act with a girl. He discovers the
antidote to his transformation potion and changes back into a
man, seeking out the aristocratic lady who rejects him since he
is now only a man. The fourth monologue is 'Ulrike Meinhof',
performed as an 'obscene tragedy' of modern times, and used to
focus attention on the Italian 'supergrass' laws for 'repentant'
terrorists.*

The Obscene Fable is a text which originated directly on the stage, quite
unexpectedly. Dario had adapted an improvised scenario from a
picaresque French fabliaux ... and called it 'The Butterfly Mouse'. He
revised and changed it for me ... I was supposed to perform it. ... The
general structure of the piece was certainly profoundly poetic, on the
same level as the best *giullarate* in *Mistero Buffo*, but certain passages
... were so crude in their erotic satire, and so ruthless in their para-
doxicality, that they made me feel uneasy. I would have had to do
violence to myself to manage to play it: the perennial condition of sexual
inhibition of a woman faced with the blackmailing myth of modesty and
shame.

Franca Rame, 'Introduction' to Il fabulazzo osceno, p. 1

The subjects dealt with in these fables are obscene in their character and
flavour. I repeat, obscene — not vulgar or scurrilous. The main aim of
the story-tellers was to overturn the idea of scandal imposed in a
terroristic way by the authorities, through a play of eroticism. Erotic
obscenity is used as a weapon of liberation. These days we could
synthesize it into an exclamation: 'Obscene is beautiful!'.

Fo, Il fabulazzo osceno, p. 5

Few of the tales that Fo recites can readily be found in books. He discovers them in obscure sources, invents details, and turns them into performance scenarios. In doing this he brings to the public some chapters of Italian history and folklore that went unrecorded because the scholars who preserved past culture favoured the ruling class; it was not in their interest for stories of political and sexual unrest to survive. ... Fo notes that popes and noblemen in the middle ages were free to write obscene literature, and circulate it among their friends, while stories for the general public survived — if they survived at all — through the oral tradition of minstrelsy in which Fo places himself. His narratives of repression and resistance to it are 'obscene' insofar as they would have been declared blasphemous or treasonous by medieval church authorities, nobility and scholars.

Schechter, 'Dario Fo's Obscene Fables', p. 87

The Open Couple

One-act comedy by Franca Rame and Dario Fo.
First production: Teatro Comunale di Monfalcone, 30 Nov. 1983
(dir. Fo; with Franca Rame); also in the U.S.A. May-June 1986, at the
Assembly Rooms, Edinburgh Festival, Aug. 1986, and
Covent Garden, Sept. 1986 (with 'The Mother' and 'The Rape'), and
in a double bill with 'A Day like Any Other', as *Parti femminili*,
Teatro Nuovo, Milan, 9 Oct. 1986).
First British production: Sir Richard Steele Pub Th., 23 Jan. 1985
(trans. Ed Emery; dir. Simon Usher).
First American production: Eureka Th. Company, San Francisco,
15 Jan. 1987 (dir. Susan Marsden).
Australian productions: Universal Th., Melbourne, 7 Jan. 1986
(dir. Lois Ellis); Zootango Th., Hobart, Tasmania, 2 Apr. 1987
(dir. Richard Davey).

Open Couple is about a couple in crisis, in which the man tries to overcome their problems with false solutions, based on a presumed notion of individual freedom, with great declarations of tolerance and rationality, as long as he is the one running the game. But it is all destined to collapse in the most dramatic way, which is grotesque at the same time, as soon as the situation is reversed and the woman communicates to her companion her own experiences, following the dictates of the mythical freedom

73

of the open couple. The man goes off his head when the woman tells him she has decided to go off with another man.

Dario Fo and Franca Rame, 'Introduction' to *Parti femminili*, p. 6

It's not a thesis play. Every line is taken from conversations we've had with our friends. It's an autobiography of the intellectuals we know, with an added surrealistic charge. The problem exists for everyone, including the working class — it's universal. The woman's role in the family situation is always one of subjugation, like the proletariat, while the man plays the role of the bourgeoisie. ... There is a tragic basis to the play which turns into comedy through the situation. ... In *Accidental Death of an Anarchist* I talked about the 'liberating belch' caused by scandal, where people's imagination creates a catharsis which distracts attention from the real political problems. In this play there's a line saying that now there's not even that belch left any more — there's no more indignation. ... In the face of the failure of revolutionary ideals, the basic problem is how people relate to one another.

Fo, in Mitchell, p. 92-3

The contribution of Franca Rame to Fo's plays has been undervalued for a long time. Even confined to the dramaturgical aspect, leaving aside her organization of a company which has always explored new avenues, and their work on stage in which her presence has always been most notable, a lot of things which have been traditionally attributed to her husband also, or even predominantly so, come from her. The political animus, or the more simply realistic aspect of Fo's company, the punctilious attention to phenomena of the real world and its stories great and small (if we can contrast this for convenience's sake with the imaginative, grotesque, story-telling and clownish attributes of Fo), is largely hers. ... This is very apparent in this piece.

Ugo Volli, *La Repubblica*, 12 Oct. 1986

Elizabeth

Two-act play.
First production: Riccione, 7 Dec. 1984 (dir. Fo).
First British production: Half Moon Th., 31 Oct. 1986
(dir. Michael Batz and Chris Bond; trans. and perf. Gillian Hanna.)
First American productions: Yale Repertory Theatre, New Haven,
1 May 1987 (trans. Ron Jenkins; dir. Anthony Taccone); Los Angeles Theater Center, 9 Oct. 1987 (dir. Arturo Corso).

The action is set over the two days of a coup d'état which the young Robert Essex, ex-lover of the queen, who is still very much in love with him, has organized to dethrone her. It is 1601 and the play is set in Elizabeth's bed chamber, which is dominated by a huge wooden horse, which the sovereign's father used to construct an equestrian statue. From the bedroom window everything that happens in the Earl of Essex's palace can be monitored. With him is Southampton, Shakespeare's patron and theatrical impresario. Elizabeth suspects that Shakespeare is not a poet who is above partisan struggles, and, out of curiosity, starts reading all his plays. The queen is quickly convinced that Shakespeare's characters are talking about her and her court. Though this applies to all the characters (she sees herself mirrored in both Richard II and Cleopatra and sees the Earl of Essex in Antony), it is with Hamlet that she finds the most profound identification, not just through precise allusions, but also in turns of phrase and mannerisms. ... Fo plays a female part, Donnazza, a type of witch whose job is to restore a youthful appearance to the queen, a highly solitary woman who is prepared to make any sacrifice to get her lover back and persuade him he is on the wrong track. Real events unfold as Shakespeare predicted: the cultivated queen is capable of great cruelty and vulgarity, as well as false madness like Hamlet, behind the arras there is always a spy or an assassin lying in ambush, and after victory over the enemy at home the more serious and definitive battle with the enemy abroad appears on the horizon: Fortinbras arrives from Norway when Hamlet dies, and James will arrive from Scotland when Elizabeth dies.

Anon. in *La Nazione*, 28 Nov. 1984

The action takes place in 1601, but its theme is very topical. It's about the commitment of the intellectual, and the need to participate in world events and take a position. It's worth stressing that it's a political play, but it's also moral, and makes a statement about the function of theatre. ... [Elizabeth's] is the first modern state. She invented the secret service and modern politics. There's even a sort of Moro affair, when three lords are kidnapped and held to ransom by rebels. She, naturally, doesn't give in to this, and maintains a hard line. ... The theatre shouldn't be regarded in an idealistic way, as if it dealt with stories that have no relation to reality. The intellectual should be committed, and so

75

much the better if he can intervene in the world around him. Authority often has very similar forms, which can be laughed at.

Fo, in *La Repubblica*, 6 Dec. 1984

Elizabeth is an excessively bawdy, vulgar comedy too fatuous to have been a revolutionary text in the early seventeenth century, too unfocused for the political satire we might expect for today. ... If we accept the premise of a deep reactionary fear of gynaeocracy, the fear that has made a harpy out of Thatcher, this is a deeply comforting piece. ... Elizabeth, to our relief, is not much more than a woman. The kindest one can say of the play is that it cuts both ways: both confirming and mocking a misogyny deeper rooted, I suspect, in Fo's native culture than our own.

Alex Renton, 'Gloriana goes for a bust job', *The Times*, 8 Nov. 1986

Problems like excessive literary references and a careless structure mar this theatrical practical joke, but Hanna's triumph is her recreation of Grossmith (superbly played by Bob Mason) speaking 'Stepney-Italian', a doggerel which sounds like a ludicrous mix of an Elizabethan Stanley Unwin and Cockney Mrs. Malaprop.

Anne McFerran, *Time Out*, 12-19 Nov. 1986

Fo's play highlights the parallels between Elizabethan imperialism and modern world politics. Some of the Queen's dialogue was taken almost verbatim from newspaper accounts of Italian political scandals. Italian audiences acknowledged the accuracy of Fo's satiric aim by punctuating their laughter with applause every time he scored a bull's eye that reminded them of current events. The parallels played themselves out so smoothly that audiences often lost track of where Elizabethan history ended and contemporary fact began. These blurred boundaries only served to reinforce Fo's contention that political injustices repeat themselves.

Ron Jenkins, 'Translator's Preface', *Elizabeth*, in *Theater*, 1987, p. 64

I know you are a sophisticated man of theatre who understands the use of allegory and anecdotes to make a point, so I don't want you to leap to any false conclusions about possible parallels between the story of Elizabeth in my play, and your own Presidency. Just because my play is about an aging leader whose advisors don't tell her what they're doing behind her back, a leader who tends to get confused and forgetful about certain details, don't think for a moment that it has anything at all to do with you. Everything in this play happened a long time ago to a queen who was at the end of her reign, and there is absolutely no parallel to the current situation in America. ... Also be assured that the minor urinary problems Elizabeth suffers in the play have nothing to do with your well publicized prostate operations, and that her obsessive concern with her image and with cosmetic beauty treatments has no relation whatsoever to the dying of your hair, your face-lifting, or the polyps that disappeared mysteriously from your nose. And don't let anyone try to convince you that Elizabeth's love for horses has anything to do with your image as a galloping cowboy. ...

> Fo, Letter to President Reagan, Prologue to American version of
> *Elizabeth*, in *Theater*, p. 66

Hellequin, Harlekin, Arlecchino

Two-act play based on *lazzi* compiled by Ferruccio Marotti and
  Delia Gambelli.
First production: Palazzo del Cinema, Venice, 18 Oct. 1985.

Four extended monologues written for the Venice Biennale on the four hundredth anniversary of the birth of Harlequin. In a lengthy 'Prologue', Marcolfa tells a story based on Giordano Bruno's play The Candlestickmaker, *about a woman who discovers her husband is having an affair with a prostitute, whom she confronts, and who teaches her her skills so she can win back her husband's sexual attention. This is repeatedly interrupted by Harlequin, who constructs a ship on stage and makes extended jokes about contemporary Italian politicians. In 'The Gravediggers', Harlequin and Razzullo are digging a grave for a suicide. They both piss in the grave, and are rebuked by a skeleton. Another skeleton appears, and the gravediggers hit and kick them. The funeral procession arrives, and a brawl breaks out, in which the dead man's brother kills the priest, and is in turn killed by the widow's lover, who dies in the process. The widow invites the gravediggers to the wake, and there is a final dance by all the dead in the graveyard.*

Act Two opens with 'The Lock': 'on one side Colombina is lovingly polishing an enormous lock. Harlequin enters on the other side with an equally enormous key, which he polishes and cuddles. He asks Colombina to let him try turning his key in her

77

lock. She gets angry at the idea of her sensitive plaything suffering such a vulgar and bulky object. They both sing the praises of their possessions; the lock belongs in heaven, and the key belongs to the emperor. But nothing can break the impasse until Colombina is hungry, and Harlequin reveals that he has a piece of bread. Colombina gives in out of hunger. The scene is played naturally, without vulgarity, and without immediately identifying the game with a sexual encounter.

Fo, in Europeo, 19 Oct. 1985, p. 63

In 'The Donkey', Harlequin is terrorized by two dogs who turn out to be Razzullo and Scaracco in masks. His girlfriend Franceschina sneers at his cowardice. He then has a long conversation with a donkey, only to discover it is again his two friends in disguise. A lion escapes from a Sultan's seraglio, and Harlequin, thinking it is his two friends playing another trick, tames it by force and impresses Franceschina. There is a final dance of animals. Two other pieces, 'Harlequin and the Flying Cat' and 'The Shepherds' Song: a Journey with the Madonna', were later discarded.

In the beginning, Harlequin was on stage for no more than a fleeting appearance. Two or three brief 'comic entrances' and that was it. If they were cut, nobody would even notice. The primordial Harlequin was a superfluous character, and the action he took part in was quite gratuitous, even senseless. What's more, his actions were horribly obscene and bloodthirsty, gratuitously violent and irrational. ... He'd come on like a mindless moron, but then he'd suddenly start philosophizing in the language of a Rabelaisian scholar. ... He was incongruous, unpredictable and absurd. ... There is no other mask in the history of the theatre in every country and epoch that can boast so many centuries of life and such success wherever he appeared. ... He was born from the commodious belly of Commedia dell'Arte, who was a real slut — one can only imagine how many lovers she had. So Harlequin has hundreds of fathers. ... We're not interested in discovering the most likely father, but in discovering his gestures, his imagination, his tricks, the games he improvised, his accidents, and to learn the hops, skips and jumps, the *lazzi*, lampoons, rambling misunderstandings, complicated deceptions, quick changes, long-winded tirades and boasts. ... If we want to be able to perform Commedia dell'Arte today, we need to improvise. ... We tried to be scientific without being stuffy. Our ambition was to concoct a show made up of fragments which are as entertaining as possible.

> Fo, 'A Mask Four Centuries Old', in
> *XXXIII Festival Internazionale del Teatro*, 1985,
> Venice Biennale, p. 46-8

In reality Fo has always been Harlequin in a sense, just as Eduardo de Filippo was always Pulcinella, in a personalized and somewhat secret way, but within a tradition. Outside Italy he is considered to be an authentic continuation of the Commedia dell'Arte, and even *Mistero Buffo* is read in this way, which is incorrect historically, but visibly real. The fact remains that Fo has always preferred to leap from the medieval *giullari* to contemporary politics, keeping his distance from the sixteenth and seventeenth centuries, the centuries of the Commedia masks.

> Volli, *Europeo*, p. 63

... *Faithful* without being philological, above all to Fo, who even recycles some of his old gags (while Rame redoes her Marcolfa), and to a certain type of theatre based on improvisation and nose-thumbing at the taboos of sex and death imposed by the powers-that-be, which after the Commedia dell'Arte became farce and variety and ended up in the cinema. When he takes off his demonic mask, Harlequin does not lose his colourfulness, and Fo's face achieves a surreal minstrelsy in a collection of pieces which is enjoyable without being earth-shattering.

> Oliviero Ponte di Pino, *Panorama*, 3 Nov. 1985

A Day Like Any Other

One-act play by Dario Fo and Franca Rame.
First production: Teatro Nuovo, Milan, 9 Oct. 1986 (as *Parti femminili*, with *The Open Couple*, dir. Fo).
First American production: Eureka Th. Company, San Francisco, 7 Jan. 1988 (trans. Christina Nutrizio and Sally Schwager; dir. Richard Seyd).

A Day Like Any Other *is, predictably, the story of an incredibly unusual day: every moment situations that are both tragic and grotesque break out. It begins with a woman in her own apartment-office making a videotape to send as a letter to her husband, whom she has lived apart from for some time. The woman warns her ex-husband that she has decided to commit suicide. Her taping of her farewell speech is interrupted by a number of telephone calls. They are the voices of women who have contacted her in the belief that they are talking to a psychoanalyst. Her phone number has been printed by mistake in a medical magazine, with the name of a famous psychiatrist who has experimented in Japan with effective methods of curing neurosis. They all ask her for advice and refuse to acknowledge the woman's protesting attempts to explain their misunderstanding. Finally our protagonist is forced, unwillingly, to accept the role of an analyst and listen to the patients' stories, which are by turns pathetic, comic and tragic. The last voice on the telephone, which to begin with sounds like the calmest, is revealed to be that of a female doctor. Our false analyst is immediately forced by the situation to assume the classic role of a 'samaritan' and try to make the 'patient' see reason and convince her not to go ahead with the insane and desperate action she is about to commit.*

Fo and Rame, 'Introduction' to *Parti femminili*, 1987, p. 5-6

Backed up by an original technological device, a telecamera which blows up the performer's image on a large screen set up on the back wall, showing Fo's intention to find new solutions for stage settings, the play combines measured doses of comedy and melancholy, wild gags and pointed social observation. Fully appropriating the language of advertising from women's magazines and daily bla bla, the text contains an exhaustive manual of current affectations, fashions, mannerisms and banalities, which accumulate obsessively to produce the paradoxical, surreal outbursts which are typical of Fo. The subject is brought to life and made concrete in human terms, and at times exhilarating, by the decisive contribution of the performer's intense stage presence. With her penitent gestures, her idiosyncratic timing and her dismay and stupefaction Rame builds up a multi-faceted portrait which expands from one invention to another into a fractured mirror-image — at times affectionate, at times cruel — of 'days like any other' in which we find ourselves involved for better or worse.

Renato Palazzi, *Corriere della sera*, 17 Oct. 1986

The Kidnapping of Francesca

Two-act play.
First production: Teatro Sloveno, Trieste, 3 Dec. 1986 (dir. Fo).

Francesca Bollini de Rill, a wealthy banker, is doing an AIDS test on a prospective young lover when kidnappers burst into her apartment disguised as firemen. She has just told her young man that she is in fact Francesca's look-alike secretary, but manages to convince the kidnappers, and the audience, that she is Francesca. They take her to a farm house in the country, wearing masks of prominent Italian politicians to disguise their identity. It transpires that they have done her a favour, since she was just about to be arrested for bankruptcy. The kidnap appears to have been organized by Francesca's lawyer and lover, whom she has instructed to give the kidnappers two billion lire ransom money. While three of the gang are collecting the money, she manages to free herself and terrorize the fourth member. In Act Two, she rings her mother, instructing her to bring two shotguns to the farm house. A priest arrives, supposedly to bless the house, and ends up performing an exorcism on the kidnapper, who has become delirious due to his torture, and has been put in the refrigerator. The mother, who is a medium, arrives and joins in until the walls of the house start caving in. The kidnappers return with the money in a suitcase, which has a bomb inside. Only Francesca knows the combination number to open it, and she refuses to do so until the kidnappers bring her their leader. This turns out to be her mother, in cahoots with Francesca's husband, who has disguised himself as the priest, and who takes over the ransom money at gunpoint. Then the real Francesca enters, revealing that the other woman is in fact her secretary, and that she has been monitoring proceedings throughout, partly through the young man. She attaches the suitcase-bomb to the ceiling, sets the timer, and exits with the young man, only to return to assure the audience that the play will not end with an explosion. She distributes the ransom money to the kidnappers, and promises them a job in her bank.

This is a play in defence of rich people. ... Of course Dario and I haven't got a very good public profile or reputation in this respect. On a number of occasions, we must admit, we've gone a bit overboard with our satire against the wealthy and powerful. But allow us to redeem ourselves. Nowadays we feel it is our duty to rush to the defence of the rich against the insane campaign which is being organized against them. ... Some people really hate and abhor the rich: magistrates, for example ... terrible examining magistrates who rise from the lower classes, and in the guise of avenging angels, beat the drum for justice being equal for all, and throw industrialists, bankers and farm owners into prison. ... Make no mistake, these days the workers have given up their class struggle, and the only ones who still carry it on, fearlessly but alone, and with great difficulty, are the employers. They never give up!

Franca Rame, *Il ratto della Francesca*, p. 18, 20

b: Other Plays

The True Story of Piero Angera, Who Wasn't at the Crusades

Three-act play, written 1960, *published* 1981.
First production: Gruppo della Tosse, Teatro Stabile, Genoa,
    21 May 1984 (dir. Tonino Conte, des. Emanuele Luzzati).

A large-cast play with songs, about the mediavel communes and the political opportunism of the crusades. Piero Angera is a scribe who finds he is able to fly, due to the purity of his thoughts. He loses this ability when he falls in love with his stepmother, the Duchess Federica. He organizes the subjects of the realm into opposition against her husband, the Duke Oddo, on his return from the crusades.

The 999th of the Thousand

One-act farce, written 1959, *published* 1976.
First production: Teatro Mobile Globo, Milan, Sept. 1959 (dir. Fo).

A 'miles gloriosus' boasts that he has taken part in the expedition of the Thousand, which he describes to his fellow townspeople in the rhetoric of military publicity. Caught out by one of Garibaldi's real soldiers, the young man is saved from disgrace by the unexpected arrival of the 'general' who pretends to recognize him, and drags him off with him for his next action.

Cappa and Nepoli, p. 44

The End of the World, or God Makes Them and Then Matches Them

Two-act play, written 1968.
Unpublished.
First production: Teatro Belli, Rome, Feb. 1979 (dir. Jose Quaglio).

Abelard and Heloise survive a world cataclysm by hiding in a sewer, and believe they are the sole remaining people in the world until they encounter a corrupt General of Intelligence and an Angel. The world is in the process of being taken over by cats in the absence of human power figures. The play deals with sexual relationships, and satirizes the 'historic compromise', in which the PCI negotiated entering the government.

The Pinball-Dummy Boss

One-act play, written 1967, *published* 1976.
First performance: in the TV show *Let's Talk About Women*, RAI TV, May 1977 (dir. Fo).

A sketch in which workers take out their feelings of aggression on a rubber dummy representing their boss. A naive female worker is persuaded to 'punish' the boss by giving him an electric shock.

On the Seventh Day God Created Prisons

Two-act play, written 1972.
Unpublished.
Unperformed.

*A direct contribution to the militant prison campaign. ... The plot is
based on one of Fo's most familiar comic schemes, the inadvertent
confusion of one person for another. A judge is called in to quell a
prison revolt; in the course of turmoil, he himself is mistaken for a
convict, beaten, and locked up. In jail, he is forced to experience
personally all the horrors which make up the daily lives of the inmates.
When an official finally discovers the mistake and procures his release,
the judge initiates such a violent, rabid campaign in denunciation of
existing prison conditions that he is assumed to be insane and is locked
up in another kind of prison — a state mental institution — for the rest
of his life.*

Suzanne Cowan, *The Militant Theatre of Dario Fo*, p. 118

Down with the Fascists!

An audiovisual show, written in 1973.
First performance: toured in factories, workers' halls, etc. in northern
　　Italy in summer, 1973, by Franca Rame and members of La Comune.
Unpublished.

*A documentary about fascism past and present, based on personal
accounts by Second World War partisans and contemporary political
militants. Includes the monologue 'Mamma Togni', later included in* The
People's War in Chile, *and urges the outlawing of fascism and the
spread of 'militant anti-fascism'.*

The Plates

One-act sketch, written 1976, *published* 1978.
First performance: In the TV show *Let's Talk About Women*, May 1977.

*An anarchic comedy in which a family, fed up with consumerism, game
shows and advertising, start throwing hundreds of plates and smashing
up their living room.*

The Giullarata

Two-act play.

First production: Palazzina Liberty, Milan, 11 Nov. 1975 (dir. Fo; with Cicciu, Concetta and Pina Busacca).

A series of songs and sketches demonstrating the art of the cantastorie *(singer-storyteller), beginning with 'The Birth of the Jongleur' from* Mistero Buffo, *and including 'The Ballad of Cicciu Corno' from* The People's War in Chile, *as well as a number of songs and sketches from Busacca's Sicilian repertoire, and songs by Fo.*

... I am a giullare cantastorie. ... The giullare strips the king, the bishops and government ministers down to their underpants with his satire. The people's laughter and sneers have always been the most dangerous threat to the authorities.

Cicciu Busacca, in *La Giullarata*, 1976, p. 19-20

The acting is done by Cicciu, who makes observations on the status and role of popular culture, quoting Brecht and stressing the connection between his ballads and the recent history of oppression. There are numerous motifs and narrative sections from Fo's repertoire in the collection. Music is the most prevalent part of the play ...

Cappa and Nepoli, p. 115

Eve's Diary

Monologue, Written 1978.
First performance: Artists' Foundation, Massachusetts, Oct. 1985
(trans. Cristina Nutrizio and Ron Jenkins; dir. Anna Maria Lisi and Ron Jenkins).
Unpublished.

A monologue based on Mark Twain's 'Diary of Adam and Eve', presenting the story of Adam and Eve from Eve's point of view.

The Tragedy of Aldo Moro

Play in one act, written and *published* in 1979.
First performance: as a reading by Fo, Palazzetto dello Sport, Padua, 21 June 1979.

85

Written in the style of a Greek tragedy, with a central situation based on
Philoctetes, *a dramatization of some of the letters Moro wrote to his*
Christian Democrat colleagues in the government while he was being
held by the Red Brigades in a 'people's prison' between March and
May in 1978. The play is set up as a forum in which Moro debates with
his colleagues, and denounces the refusal of the government to
negotiate with the Red Brigades as a desire to make Moro a scapegoat.
The play is presented by a Jester and there are dances by Satyrs and
Bacchanals. Fo discarded the play after only one reading.

I have been working on the Moro play for a long time now, but I have
had great difficulty finding a direction and a style for the second act,
because current events keep on overtaking the development of the play.
The powers-that-be are continually attempting to mystify the issues
involved, and cover them in dust. They are cleverer than I am, and
always one step ahead of me. However, the political situation since the
death of Moro has developed exactly as as I predicted in the play. But
I am left with a format —that of Greek tragedy — fifteen characters, but
no performance date.

Fo, Interview on RAI Radio 3, 17 Oct. 1979

Patapumfete

A clown show in two parts, written in 1982.
Unpublished.

Seven clown routines (including 'The Morality of the Blind Man and the
Cripple' from Mistero Buffo) *written for the Colombaioni brothers.*

The Candlestickmaker

A monologue, written 1983.
Unpublished and unperformed.

A sketch loosely based on the general situation of Giordano Bruno's
sixteenth-century comedy of the same name, and used in a modified
form in Elizabeth *and* Harlequin. *A dresser informs the audience that*
the play they are about to see has been called off due to the illness of
the leading actress, and begins telling them the story. A candlemaker

has grown tired of his wife and begun to frequent a prostitute. The wife approaches the prostitute, who trains her in her art, enabling the husband to rediscover his wife as a prostitute.

God Makes Them and Then Murders Them

Two-act play, written 1984.
Unpublished and unperformed.

Written ...in the light of the new wave of revelations about the Mafia and its activities at the centre of power politics ... a wide-ranging satirical farce in the style of ... Fo's plays of the 1960s. All the characters reveal an identity different from the one they claim to be, and are involved in criminal gangs connected with top-level politicians (there is a 'quasi' Andreotti in the play). The comic climax is reached by way of a grotesque device (involving a fake castration), a tour de force which takes place in the lounge of a famous criminal surgeon. It is a play of masks, involving a comic situation based on misunderstanding. Towards the end the rival criminal organizations form a consortium ... and set the surgeon up as a scapegoat. He objects, and the farce ends in a general massacre. But first the action is interrupted to accommodate a brief discussion among the actors as to whether it is legitimate to present all the characters as either negative or corrupt.
Bent Holm, *The World Turned Upside Down*, p. 32

c: Adaptations

I Think Things Out and Sing Them for You

'A Popular Representation in two acts based on original material edited by Cesare Bermani and Franco Coggiola.'
First production: Il Gruppo Nuovo Canzoniere Italiano, Teatro Carignano, Turin, 16 Apr. 1966 (dir. Fo). Second Edition by Nuova Scena, Camera di Lavoro, Sala di Vittorio, Milan, 8 Apr. 1969. Third Edition by La Comune, Teatro della Gioventu, Genoa, 27 Feb. 1973.

A show based on about a hundred traditional Italian workers' and

*peasant songs from various different regions which were researched by
Il Nuovo Canzoniere, and choreographed by Fo. 'In the first part,
popular traditions, festivals and the war seen from the point of view of
the lower classes were brought to life with very precise rhythms. The
second part was glossier, and included a series of beautiful paintings
which showed the intuitions of Fo the painter, with the work of washer-
women, a wedding, the passion of Christ according to apocryphal
gospels, ending in a great crescendo with the popular anarchist song
Our Home is the Whole Wide World", sung by everyone at the top of
their voices, often with ... the audience joining in.'*

Valentini, p. 98-9

*The second edition of the show, performed without Il nuovo canzoniere,
included about a dozen songs written by Fo, like 'I Saw a King' (later
recorded by Enzo Jannacci) and 'Don't Wait for St. George'. The third
edition included the Sicilian cantastorie Cicciu Busacca, and some
Sicilian material which was later used in* The Giullarata.

We were constantly concerned with philological precision, out of respect
for the material, which we wanted to use as it was. We were worried that
altering the songs would mean that their class point of view would not
be so predominant. Dario's concern was with trying to pull the songs
apart and make them more theatrical. We were constantly running into
obstacles; we refused to do things which seemed absurd to us at the
time, like putting on make-up and moving to a theatrical rhythm.

Ivan della Mea, in Valentini, p. 97

'If we don't know where we come from it's impossible for us to know
where we're going' said Gramsci; but every time there is any serious
proposal to do research into the people and history which really
overturns the 'false culture' that bourgeois education has perpetrated for
centuries, then you see a lot of 'revolutionaries' turning up their
noses. ... The bosses aren't producers, they don't cut cane, they don't
make ladders or build walls and so when they have to fight on territory
and with rules set up by the people, they always lose ...

Fo, 'Towards an Introduction to an Essay on Popular Culture',
Ciragiono e canto 3, 1973, p. 89, 98

The Sunday Walk

Two-act play by Georges Michel, translated from the French and
adapted by Dario Fo.

First production: Teatro Durini, Milan, 18 Jan. 1967 (dir. Fo).

The Sunday Walk was a fable about petit bourgeois apathy represented by the Sunday walk of a family pursuing its little myths and well-being oblivious to the violence and massacres in the world around it, which in the original play were the Algerian War and the OAS. In Fo's rewritten version, these becme clashes between police and demonstrators, and the Americans in Vietnam. The modifications which Fo made to the text were not restricted to political allusions. Michel's play was adapted, its provocative elements accentuated, and any residue of pathos was eliminated.

Valentini, p. 101

The Soldier's Tale

'Stage Action by Dario Fo with music by Stravinsky (Histoire du Soldat, Octet).'
First production: for Il Teatro alla Scala, Teatro Ponchielli, Cremona, 18 Nov. 1978 (dir. Fo).

A free adaptation of Ramuz' libretto for Stravinsky's chamber opera, turning it into a 'choral' political satire about migration from the south of Italy, with grammelot and a cast of 32 students from La Scala instead of the four in the original version. The soldier-protagonist is played as a kind of zanni, by a number of different actors, and there is a series of large-scale stage 'pictures' of the city, the stock exchange, war, a market, and a 'ship of fools', as well as a gigantic cane puppet.

The Opera of Guffaws

Adapted from John Gay's *The Beggar's Opera* and some ideas by Jacopo Fo.
First production: Teatro Il Fabbricone, Prato, 1 Dec. 1981 (dir. Fo). Revised edition, Teatro Nazionale, Milan, Apr. 1982 (with Fo as Peachum).

Originally an adaptation of Brecht's Threepenny Opera *commissioned but rejected by the Berliner Ensemble, Fo later based the play more on*

Gay's original play. A rock opera, with songs based on motifs from Jimi Hendrix, Janis Joplin, Bob Dylan, etc., in which Macheath becomes a Mafioso-type financial criminal, Peachum runs a fraud agency for drug addicts, drop-outs and social security dodgers, and there is satire on mechanization, electrical appliances, drugs, sex and violence. Lockit becomes associated with Lockheed, and Macheath's escape from prison takes place during the Notting Hill Carnival.

The Barber of Seville

An adaptation of the opera by Rossini.
First production: Amsterdam Musiktheater, 24 Mar. 1987 (dir. Fo, music dir. Richard Buckley).

A version of Rossini's opera directed and designed by Fo, with a Commedia dell'Arte troupe added to the singers.

... This particular opera — or the Beaumarchais play on which it is based — does have a kind of relationship with the Commedia dell'Arte, and so has Dario Fo. ... The trouble is that like most producers coming fresh to opera, particularly comic opera, Dario Fo has no faith in the music as being worthy of attention in itself. ... Fo will do anything — fly a kite, paddle a gondola, sit on a swing, toss a doll in a blanket — anything to distract his audience from Rossini.

Gerald Larner, *The Guardian*, 26 Mar. 1987

d: Films

The Screwball (Lo svitato)

Released 1956 (dir. Carlo Lizzani, screenplay by Fo and Lizzani, starring Fo and Rame).

Fo plays 'Achilles, a Hulot-like factotum for an evening newspaper, who travels around looking for a scoop in the Milan of the "economic miracle".'

Cappa and Nepoli, p. 22

A satirical film which misses all its probable targets.

Tullio Kezich, *Sipario*, quoted in Valentini, p. 53

The only film I made of any value ... [it] had its defects, but its comedy was too unusual in comparison with the low-level sort that predominated at the time. It was a precursor of Woody Allen and surreal comedy. It had the lowest box office takings of that year, and despite being a fiasco, it had pieces of good cinema in it, as is proved by the fact that it is now in the cinetèques.

Franca Rame, *Domenica del Corriere*, 3 Oct. 1981, p. 44

Fo also collaborated on the screenplays of *Souvenir d'Italie* (dir. Antonio Pietrangeli, 1957), *Rascel Fifì* (dir. Guido Leoni, 1957, with Franca Rame), and *Nata a marzo* (*Born in March*, dir. Pietrangeli, 1958)

For me the lesson of the cinema meant learning from a technical point of view what people had already grasped: a story divided into sequences, a fast pace, sharp dialogue, and getting rid of the conventions of space and time. Working on screenplays gave me an apprenticeship as a playwright and I was able to transfer the lessons of the new technical means into the theatre.

Fo, in Valentini, p. 55

e: Radio Plays

Poor Dwarf (Poer nano)

Eighteen monologues written and performed by Fo on RAI Radio, weekly from Dec. 1951.

Fo also participated in the scripting and performance of two other radio comedy series: *Chichiricchi* (1952-53, with Giustino Durano), in which Fo created the character of the civil servant Gorgogliati; and an eleven-part series called *You Don't Live on Bread Alone* (1955, with Franco Parenti).

At that time I wasn't used to performing a written text. At the most I jotted down a scenario or a few notes. I wasn't used to the literary dimension. And in fact it was absent from these texts. They were full of inserts, expressions in Lombard dialect, back-tracking, and comments on situations. it was an expression of a tradition which had never been written down, and for which it was necessary to re-invent a form of writing.

Fo, interview with Enzo Magri, in Valentini, p. 36

f: Television Plays

Who's Seen It? (Chil'ha visto?)
Canzonissima

Who's Seen It? transmitted by RAI 2, 1962.
Canzonissima transmitted by RAI 1, 1962.

A series of sketches and songs transmitted in one programme on RAI 2 and in eight parts on RAI 1. The theme song to Canzonisima *was 'Children of the Economic Miracle', and other songs included 'That Ugly City of Mine', about Milan. The sketches satirized the entertainment industry, industrial accidents, the Mafia, conditions in prisons and mental institutions, scandals and corruption, industrial relations and building speculation. In one sketch, Fo was 'arrested' by two 'policemen' for breaches of censorship. The programme was taken off after the eighth episode, when Fo and Rame refused to drop a sketch referring to a current strike, and they were effectively banned from Italian TV for fourteen years.*

There was one sketch which caused an avalanche of protest. It showed a worker who was in the habit of kissing the effigy of his boss as if it were a saint. This worker had a fat aunt who weighed a ton, and who came to visit him one day in the factory. It was a canned meat factory. The aunt tripped and fell into a machine, and came out as mincemeat because they couldn't stop the production line. The worker was given 150 cans of meat which he kept in a cupboard at home and showed to his friends every so often, telling them 'this is my aunt'. ... There were a lot of complaints against this from meat producers and industrialists, but none from aunts.

Fo, *La Repubblica*, 24-25 Apr. 1977

Before *Canzonissima* we did a show for the second channel called

Who's Seen It? which very few people saw, but in which we were allowed to say virtually whatever we liked. Then to show that TV was open to the left, since there was a centre-left government, they asked us to do *Canzonissima.* ... We got to the eighth episode. We had already done programmes on the Mafia, and the toll-keepers, which had caused a lot of fuss, because the Mafia was, and still is, very powerful, and the toll-keepers were on strike. In the eighth episode there was to be a sketch about the building trade, about deaths and the indifference of bosses to the excessive number of work accidents. The TV channel said no to that piece, and to two others in the same episode. They even said they couldn't understand why we were so stubborn about defending them: they weren't even funny.

Rame, Domenica del Corriere, 3 Oct. 1981, p. 45

Let's Talk about Women

Transmitted: RAI 2 in two parts, 18 and 20 May 1977, as part of two retrospective 'cycles' of Fo's plays in the Spring and Autumn of 1977, recorded live with audiences in the Palazzina Liberty. (Other plays televised were *Mistero Buffo, Throw the Lady Out, Isabella, Three Sailing Ships and a Con Man, Seventh Commandment, Steal a Bit Less* and *I Think Things Out and Sing Them for You.*)

A series of songs, sketches and pieces from other Fo plays, like the monologues 'Michele Lu Lanzone' and 'Mamma Togni'. The programme also included the short farce 'The Plates' and 'Waking Up'. In 'The Creation', the first woman immediately kneels in submission to the first man; in 'The Holy Family' the roles of Mary and Joseph are reversed, with Joseph riding the donkey; St. Augustine expresses his bewilderment about the existence of a female soul; the use of boys for female roles in the Elizabethan theatre is satirized; Fo boycotts Rame when she attempts to sing the feminist song 'Io sono mia' (I am Mine); Rame sings a blues song which is completely upstaged by Fo's accompaniment. A wealthy industrialist who is anti-abortion becomes pregnant through a process of parthogenesis. His wife and daughter are also pregnant, and he decides to have an abortion.

Buona sera con Franca Rame

Twenty half-hour programmes written and directed by Fo, transmitted on RAI 2 from Dec. 1979 to Jan. 1980.

In between the opening song, a satirical reversal of 'Little Red Riding Hood' in which the wolf is kidnapped and held to ransom, and the closing song by Fo satirizing UFOs and superheroes as devices to distract people's attention from social and political problems, a series of satirical songs and sketches, including one on the charges against Social Democrat Defence Minister Tanassi for fraud and corruption in the Lockheed affair, and his 're-education' by Rame.

The Tricks of the Trade

Six one-hour programmes, transmitted on RAI 3, Feb-Mar. 1985.

A live recording of the performance-seminars Fo gave at the Teatro Argentina in Rome in October 1984.

Forced Transmission

Eight ninety-minute programmes, transmitted on RAI 3,
     12 Apr.-31 May 1988 (dir. Alida Fanoli).

A variety series incorporating new satirical sketches about RAI television, Italian politicians and topical events like the celebration of Liberation Day on 25 April together with items from Fo and Rame's repertoire such as We Won't Pay! *and* The Bologna Riot. *Also includes exerpts from Fo and Rame's 'banned' 1962 TV series* Canzonissima *and Rame's 'Buona Sera con Franca Rame', a number of Fo's 'grammelots', and songs by Enzo Jannacci, with whom Fo collaborated as a songwriter in the 1950s.*

In Britain, the Belt and Braces version of *Accidental Death of an Anarchist* was broadcast on Channel Four on 14 Sept. 1983, while a one-hour programme, 'Dario Fo', directed by Dennis Marks, was shown in the BBC 2 Arena series on 26 Feb. 1984. This included parts of 'The Resurrection of Lazarus' and 'Boniface VIII'. Channel Four also broadcast a programme, directed by Stuart Hood, entitled 'Dario Fo: Modern Jester', in December 1985, in which John McGrath and Griff Rhys Jones discussed sections of *Mistero Buffo* from the RAI TV cycle.

a: Songs

Dario Fo, *Ballate e canzoni*, Bertani, Verona, 1974.
  Second ed., Newton Compton, Rome, 1976.

Anthology of the texts of songs from Fo's plays, 1953 to 1973.

b: Prose Writings

Don't Tell Me about Arches, Tell Me about Your Prisons

Edited by Franca Rame, F. R. Edizioni, 1984.

A book based on the diaries kept by the mother of Alberto Buonoconto, a member of NAP (Armed Proletarian Nucleus) who went insane and committed suicide at the age of 27, after being subjected to years of imprisonment in various jails all over Italy on the basis of scant evidence and charges of possession of arms and false documents.

A Short Manual for the Actor

Turin, Einaudi, 1987). With a section by Franca Rame.

A transcript of various seminar-workshops which Fo has given in the 1980s, particularly 'The Tricks of the Trade', 'The History of Masks' and the Riverside Workshops, and workshops held at the Free University of Alcatraz in Santa Cristina, Perugia. Divided into six Days, it covers Commedia dell'Arte, the Rame family, the theatrical text, Diderot, masks, gestures, laughter, songs, dance, movement, mime, breaking the fourth wall, grammelot, the giullari, *theatre of situation, the role of the spectator, theatre of commitment, filmic aspects of theatre perspective (with illustrations from* Tale of a Tiger)*, make-up, ancient Greek theatre, the voice, improvisation, clowns, theatre and literature, epic theatre, female clowns, women in theatre, and a glossary of theatrical terms.*

Origins (1960)

I'm sure that everything starts from where you're born. In my case, I was born in a little town on Lake Maggiore, near the Swiss border. A town of smugglers and fishermen who were virtually smugglers. Two professions which require a great deal of imagination as well as a good dose of courage. It's a well-known fact that people who use their imagination to break the law always keep a certain amount in reserve for their own pleasure and to entertain their close friends. Growing up in this environment, where everybody was a character, and every character was on the lookout for a good story, I was able to go into the theatre with a fairly unusual repertoire which was lively, relevant and real in the way that stories invented by real people are real.

In Lanfranco Binni, *Attento te!*, p. 193

The New and the Old (1967)

I maintain that in the theatre, the more one approaches the new by way of experimentation, the more there is a need to seek out roots in the past, by which I mean the relevant aspects of the past — above all those which are attached to the roots of the people, which derive from the people's manifestations of life and culture ... and which enable the expression of new research and new investigations on the basis of the 'new within the traditional'.

In Valentini, p. 99

The Fabulatori (Story-Tellers) (1969)

They went around Lake Maggiore where I lived, performing in the piazzas and *osterie*, telling strange stories, partly naive and partly crazy. Their main feature was simplicity. Their stories were simple hyperboles based on an observation of everyday life, but behind these 'absurd' stories they hid a bitterness; the bitterness of disappointed people, and a biting satire against the official world which probably few people picked up on.

Interview with Cesare Furnari, in Binni, p. 194

Architecture (1969)

When I was studying architecture I got interested in Romanesque churches. I was amazed how such powerful works were the expression not of intellectuals or artists with a capital A, but of simple sculptors, workers and builders who were ignorant and illiterate. I suddenly discovered a new and real culture; the creative power of people who have always been defined as 'simple' and 'ignorant', and have always been the 'pariahs' of official culture.

Interview with Furnari

Satire (1970)

As far as a preoccupation with ridicule, laughter, sarcasm, irony and the grotesque is concerned, I have to say — I'd be a liar if I said otherwise — it's my job. I've been teaching this lesson for years — the origins of the grotesque and the significance of the grotesque in Marxist and pre-Marxist culture and irony.

To take just one example — Brecht. Brecht says that the highest manifestation of satire — which is making people conscious, because it burns down to the deepest level — is precisely the manifestation of the grotesque. That is to say nothing gets down into the mind and the intelligence as deeply as satire. ... The best didactic lessons of Marxism should be confronted by this fact. ...

The end of satire is the first alarm bell signalling the end of real democracy. The person who said that really knew what he was talking about. That was Mayakovsky. ... If you only believe in the revolution if you keep a straight face, with no irony, no grotesqueness, then I don't believe in it. Irony has always been an explosion of liberation. But if we want to be 'illuminated' and negate the importance of the *giullare*, of making people laugh about the conditions they are subjected to ... well, we're not even Marxists ...

'Dialogue with an Audience', p. 16

Throw-away Theatre (1974)

Our theatre is a throw-away theatre (*un teatro da bruciare*), a theatre which won't go down in bourgeois history, but which is useful, like a newspaper article, a debate or a political action.

Interview in *Playboy*, quoted in Binni, p. 385

Breaking the Fourth Wall (1974)

When we've reached the point where we agree we need to break down the fourth wall, we find ourselves completely opposed to the idea of identifying the actor with the character: the actor is *me*, I try to identify with him, find inside myself all the fripperies, the innards, all my defects, all my qualities, in an attempt to dress up the character as myself. That's what Stanislavsky's all about, and it's the worst type of reactionary, conservative, bourgeois position ...

If instead I try to create the vision of a community, a chorus, a communion, obviously I'm not going to be too concerned about talking about myself — I'm talking about collective problems. If I seek out collective problems, what I'm saying and the language I use will be different; it'll be forced to be epic. This is why all the popular theatre is always epic, because it's based on a clear ideological fact — the ideology of community, of a communion of interests, social interests, interests of living together, producing together, and sharing the proceeds.

'Popular Culture', p. 52

Political Theatre (1977)

The expression 'political theatre' is very misleading — one immediately thinks of Piscator's 'political theatre'. Piscator, however, used the term to provoke controversy. It was part of a polemic against 'théâtre digestif' — a theatre which had become remote due to contingent dramatic and lyrical problems. Piscator's theatre was political in the sense of being run directly by the working class.

In using the term 'political' today, I don't want to raise people's hackles. This happens, quite justifiably, because political theatre has become a sort of subtitle for boring theatre — non-entertaining theatre. It goes without saying that all theatre, and all art, is political. The very attempt to hide its political value, as in Feydeau, gives rise to the most overt political theatre which deals with the politics of a certain social class, in this case the bourgeoisie. ...

So when we say political theatre, we're adding a useless defining adjective. This is acceptable as a kind of polemic label contrasting with theatre conceived as an all-embracing form of artistic enlightenment. I prefer to call the plays performed by La Comune popular theatre, because of their content and their concern with retrieving a class-based theatre.

'Some Aspects of Popular Theatre', p. 132

Theatre of Situation (1977)

Theatre of situation ... is not a term I've invented: it was established by Meyerhold and Brecht. In this type of theatre it is the situation which determines the development of the action, by way of the interplay and the clash between the characters. But it isn't just the characters, with their stories, their concerns, their faces, or their *vis*, as the French say, who determine this development. Molière's theatre is a theatre of situation, Ruzante's theatre is a theatre of situation, all popular theatre is a theatre of situation. ... In *Accidental Death of an Anarchist*, for example, the situation is an actual event. Just as in Ruzante there's a return from war, here there's a maniac who gets inside a police station and puts the police on trial, reversing the usual process. The situation is fundamental because it deals with actuality — the state killing an individual, fabricating a whole mechanism, placing bombs, causing a slaughter, finding the guilty party, killing him, and then continuing to perpetrate violence and oppression.

'Some Aspects of Popular Theatre', p. 132-3

Fishing for Laughs (1977)

The comic fishes for laughs by virtually throwing out a comic line, or a hook, into the audience. He indicates where the audience's reaction has to be gathered in and also virtually where the hook is cast, because otherwise the tension built up between stage and audience would die down. Winding in the hook doesn't mean snuffing out the audience reaction, but correcting its flow with a flick of the rod. The comic's ability lies in knowing that if he carries on for a while on the same tack he'll snap the audience's capacity to keep up with his theme. So he breaks into stage action, using something extraneous (a spectator's funny way of laughing, for example ...). Then the comic casts out the hook again, for a bigger laugh (although he can fish for laughs by casting out the hook more than once before provoking one big laugh). ... The audience's real way of laughing can be divided into two types: when it is symptomatic of involvement in the play and when it is not. The difference lies between the mechanical reaction of laughing and the relationship through which an audience collaborates in building the play. ... All popular theatre requires the audience to be 'inside', and take part in the rhythm of laughter.

Artese, p. 53-5

Brecht and Epic Theatre (1977)

Brecht's epic theatre is epic in its form, not in its effective result. It involves the audience through their brains, not through the elements of the play: laughter, booing, gasping, presentiment and discomfort. Brecht's epic theatre requires characters to be represented rather than interpreted, because it requires the creation of a critical distance from them by the audience. Our comic theatre uses these techniques, it's true, but it doesn't pose the problem of the actor's detachment from the character: comic actors have to live the part on stage (I am not talking about roles). ...If they believe in the reason behind the comedy, they cannot avoid identifying with the different comic situations they are involved in. These reasons are for me and my colleagues the same reasons that we work in the theatre.

Artese, p. 57

Comedy and Pathos (1977)

For ... a lot of people the comic must absolutely be a sad character. This is a romantic, manneristic ideal, the 'vesti la giubba e la faccia infarina' (from *I Pagliacci*: 'Put on the costume and put flour on your face'), the Pierrot who is forced to make people laugh but whose heart is full of grief. But above all, the comic must be 'solo'. This is an absurdity; it is the negation of theatre, where the laughter, applause, murmuring and silence of the audience have always been an integral part of performance. The presence of the audience is the musical counterpoint in the context of the performance. ... Often literary authors try to write plays without realizing that a play-text is a score, with its own rhythm, silences and pauses.

Valentini, p. 177-8

Christ and the Giullari (1977)

... When I began to study the history of the theatre, and research its origins, I noticed that most [early theatre] texts were based on religious stories. It was impossible to revive the theatre of the *Giullari* without coming to terms with Christianity, its protagonists, and its temporal power. So bit by bit, over the years I put together this show which has as its protagonist Christ, the apostles and the Madonna, and where saints, miracles and the gospels come into play. Not because, as many people wondered, I had become a Christian. I have always been an atheist, a Marxist and a confirmed materialist, and I will continue to be. But in my research into medieval texts I came across this figure of Christ, transformed by the people into a kind of hero against the authorities and church hierarchies, too often to be able to ignore him ... a different, more humane Christ, always on the side of the underdogs. He possesses a pagan, almost Dionysiac joy for love, festivity, beauty and worldly things. At the same time he is full of hatred and violence towards hypocritical priests, the aristocracy who tried to lord it over the poor, and the arrogance of the church and its temporal power. This probably isn't the Christ of history, but it is the Christ produced by the great cultural tradition of the people. In fact people today understand him immediately, without any need for explanations. They acknowledge him as part of their culture and recognize him.

Valentini, p. 176-7

Theatre of Intervention (1978)

The type of theatre I would like to propose has two directions. First, theatre as a retrieval of medieval peasant culture, linked to the important moments of our history, and tied up with class struggle, religious conflicts and so on. Second, theatre as counter-information about the events which occur in our social reality: exposing the violence of the system, police oppression, and using the grotesque and satire in such a way that the comedian's distorting lens enables the public to experience a synthesizing, didactic vision, which means giving them alternatives or moments of critical reflection, etc.

Another fundamental aspect of this kind of theatre is that it is the result of a debate: it doesn't rain down vertically on people's heads, but when it is performed it has already been digested and debated, and has even created conflicts and arguments. This means that the audience is directly involved in the play, modifying it and suggesting changes — the play is part of the audience's reality.

'Some Aspects of Popular Theatre', p. 136

Terrorism (1980)

Terrorism never destabilizes the established rule; rather it strengthens it, since it destabilizes the opposition (even when the opposition is most moderate) which is thus forced, in order to avoid being suspiciously drawn in as a cover to terrorism, to accept, support and allow those laws and those uncontrollable, violent acts which will in fact be used against citizens and workers (and their class warfare), not to mention the spontaneous movements of those who have been deceived. ...

The solution to the problem is of no interest to Power or the Power Party. What interests them is the spectacle and the emotional participation of the spectator citizen in a continuous merry-go-round of bombastic facts, much like a television 'mystery' where everyone is the suspect, everyone is the murderer — the accomplice — the instigator — the terrorist — the right-hand man. Even if it cannot be proved that he or she is guilty, anymore, nobody is ever left innocent. ... Before this spectacle, we most resemble the unwary dullard at a play, who does not see the ropes and is amazed by a flying aureole. ... You too can play this game of uncovering the fraud.

'The Sandstorm Method', trans. Peter Caravetta,
James Cascaito and Lawrence Venuiti, p. 214-16

Improvisation (1983)

People think that Franca and I leave a very wide leeway for improvisation, and that the structure of our performance is left entirely to chance and some whim of the moment, or the 'state of grace' that may sustain us one night but desert us the next. Nothing could be further from the truth. Our technique of improvisation is connected to a scientific method which has very precise rules and professional codes. This means that the basic nature of our performance is fairly constant. It varies only according to the amount of preparation we have done, or the charge the audience gives us or takes from us. But in the end we're always the ones who lead the dance.

'The Professional Actor', unpublished manuscript, 1983, p. 2

Collaboration (1985)

The values of our society were established by men and male writers. I am a writer insofar as I am an author, whereas Franca, although she is an author of a lot of her own work, is put in second place because it is thought that she only writes because of my existence and that I am a kind of chaperon. A bit like the maestro who allows his concubine, even if she's his wife, to avail herself of a bit of satisfaction. This is the result of a lack of civilization which derives from a long-established and fundamentally male sexist attitude. ... Franca is very important in my work. She organizes everything with great imagination, invention and talent, and organization is one of the basic aspects of our work. She also makes decisions about plays. I get very angry when she censures me, but I've often had to concede she is right. She has a sixth sense ...

Interview with Catherine Spaak, *Moda Italia*, Sept. 1985, p. 341

Mime and Lecoq (1987)

The art of mime is the art of communicating by synthesis, not of slavishly imitating natural gestures ... but of alluding, indicating, implying and making people imagine. The theatre is a fiction based on reality, not an imitation. ...

From our first collaboration thirty years ago, I clashed with Lecoq over the ideological as well as the dramaturgical dimension which was necessary to the craft of mime. ... These clashes have always occurred on a level of complete mutual respect, and there is still a profound friendship between us. ... Lecoq's mimes are all identical, whether they are Japanese or Americans from Massachusetts, or Filipino or from Bergamo. They are also unable to get rid of the mechanical, stereotyped gestures they have learned.

It is dangerous to learn techniques slavishly without deciding first what moral context they are to be placed in. It's like learning how to build a house piece by piece, its stressed structures and superstructures, without ever worrying about where it is going to be built, on what territory or in what environment, on a rocky slope or in a swamp.

Manuale, p. 229, 234, 235

Commedia dell'Arte (1987)

With regard to reading the Commedia dell'Arte, I have discovered that it is not enough just to stick to the usual manuals on the subject. One has to immerse oneself in real research into defining and deciphering the scenarios, which are numerous, comparing and contrasting them with one another, especially from the point of view of interpreting the *lazzi*, which is a real mystery; and comparing them with the comic devices of the so-called minor theatre: the popular farces of the eighteenth and nineteenth century, variety, *avanspettacolo*, clown routines and even the comedy of the silent cinema. It is in these forms of comedy that a lot of the Commedia dell'Arte material has come down.

Manuale, p. 109-10

Foreign Productions (1987)

I often notice that Franca's and my plays are put on only because they are good box office, it's not as if the directors, producers and principal actors come and say 'I'm only putting on your play because it works and it's entertaining, I couldn't give a damn about the moral and ideological arguments you've put into it.' No, to hear them it would seem that all they are interested in is the message, the political content. That is where the deception occurs. Unfortunately, after a company has already opened, one can hardly take on the responsibility of throwing all the actors and technicians out into the street ... quite apart from the fact that the laws regarding authors' rights have all sorts of loopholes. Luckily this is not always the case: there are a lot of companies, like the Berliner Ensemble or [Gavin Richards's] group who put on *Anarchist* in London, or the co-operative directed by Echantillon in France or the San Francisco Mime Troupe who, although they use stylized forms which I don't find entirely convincing, have put on our plays very 'cleanly' and stylishly. They are above all fairly consistent in what they do.

The main defect I often notice in productions of most of our plays outside Italy is an excess of colour. They all tend to be overloaded with effects, and stuffed full of gratuitous and irrelevant gags; there is no realization that with some plays where the situation works in a way which is comic in itself, nothing, or at most a minimal addition is needed to make it entertaining. There is almost never any restraint or the slightest detachment in the way the lines are played. Jouvet's motto can be applied to them: 'Ils jouent tous les repliques'. (They play all the cues.) They also put all sorts of expressionistic make-up on their faces, with variations according to the current fashion, which is completely off the mark ... they 'grimace' and splutter and muck up all the lines. I have no idea how they can manage to be successful despite all this. Perhaps there is something miraculous about our plays which we haven't even noticed.

Manuale, p. 249-50

a: Primary Sources in English

Plays

Accidental Death of an Anarchist, trans. with Introduction by Suzanne Cowan, in *Theater*, X, No. 2, Spring 1979.

Ulrike Meinhof and *Tomorrow's News*, trans. with Introduction by Tony Mitchell, in *Gambit*, IX, No. 36, 1980.

Female Parts, trans. Margaret Kunzle, adapt. Olwen Wymark, with Introduction by Stuart Hood, Pluto, 1981; Methuen, 1987.

About Face, trans. with Introduction by Dale McAdoo and Charles Mann, in *Theater*, XIV, No. 3, Summer/Fall 1983.

Trumpets and Raspberries, trans. and adapt. R. C. McAvoy and Anna-Maria Giugni, with Introduction by Stuart Hood, Pluto, 1984; Methuen, 1987.

Orgasmo Adulto Escapes from the Zoo, trans. and adapt. Estelle Parsons, Broadway Play Publications, 1984.

We Won't Pay! We Won't Pay!, 'North American Version' by R. G. Davis, Samuel French, New York, 1984.

An Open Couple — Very Open, trans. Stuart Hood, in *Theater*, XVII, No. 1, Winter 1985. With *An Ordinary Day*, Methuen, forthcoming.

Accidental Death of an Anarchist, trans. Gillian Hanna, adapt. Gavin Richards, with Introduction by Stuart Hood, Pluto, 1980; revised edition, Methuen, 1987.

Archangels Don't Play Pinball, trans. R. C. McAvoy and Anna-Maria Giugni, ed. and introduced by Stuart Hood, Methuen, 1987.

Elizabeth: Almost by Chance a Woman, trans. and adapt. Gillian Hanna, ed. and introduced by Stuart Hood, Methuen, 1987; American version, trans. with Introduction by Ron Jenkins, in *Theater*, Summer/Fall 1987.

Can't Pay? Won't Pay!, trans. Lino Pertile, adapt. Bill Colvill and Robert Walker, with Introduction by Stuart Hood and Franca Rame, Methuen, 1988.

Mistero Buffo, trans. Ed Emery, ed. and introduced by Stuart Hood, Methuen, 1988.

The following plays, all translated by Ed Emery, are published by Theatretexts, 1 Branch Road, London E14:
One Was Nude and One Wore Tails, *The Good that a Burglar can Bring*, *Corpse for Sale*, *Housepainters Have*

No Memories, Women Undressed and Bodies to be Despatched, He Who Steals a Foot is Lucky in Love, The Comic Mysteries, Michele Lu Lanzone, I'd Rather Die Tonight If I Had to Think It Had All Been in Vain, Fedayin, The Tale of a Tiger, The Opera of Guffaws, Coming Home, The Mother, The Rape, The Open Couple, The Butterfly Mouse, Isabella.

Articles and Documents

'Dialogue with an Audience' (translated by Tony Mitchell), *Theatre Quarterly,* Vol. IX, No. 35, Autumn 1979, p. 11-16.
'The Sandstorm Method' (translated by Peter Caravetta, James Cascaito and Lawrence Venuti), *Semiotext(e)*, Vol. III, No. 3, 1980. p. 214-16. (On terrorism.)
Dario Fo and Franca Rame Theatre Workshops at Riverside Studios, London, 28 April, 5, 12, 13, and 19 May 1983 (including texts of *Waking Up, I Don't Move, I Don't Scream, My Voice is Gone,* and *The Mother*, trans. Jytte Lollesgard), Red Notes, London, 1983.
'Popular Culture' (translated by Tony Mitchell), *Theater*, Vol. XIV, No. 3, Summer/Fall 1983, p. 50-4. (Also in an abbreviated version in *Trumpets and Raspberries*, op. cit.)
'When They Beat Us, We Suffer', *Index on Censorship*, Vol. XIV, No. 1, 1985, p. 59. (On censorship in Italy and the USA.)
'Aspects of Popular Theatre' (translated by Tony Mitchell), *New Theatre Quarterly*, Vol. I, No. 2, May 1985, p. 204-16. (Contains 'Theatre of Situation' and 'Retrieving the Past, Exposing the Present'.)
'Toto: the Violence of the Marionette and the Mask' (translated by Stuart Hood), *Theater,* Summer/Fall, 1987, p. 6-12. (On the famous Italian comic.)

Interviews

Luigi Ballerini and Giuseppe Risso, 'Dario Fo Explains' (translated by Lauren Hallquist and Fiorenza Weinpple), *The Drama Review*, Vol. XXII, No. 1, Mar. 1978, p. 34-48. (An overview of Fo's work to 1978 and the return to TV, *Throw the Lady Out*.)
Catherine Itzin, 'The "How-To" of Political Theatre', *Tribune*, 14 Mar. 1980, p. 9. (On *Accidental Death of an Anarchist* and *Mother's Marijuana*.)
David Groves, 'Fo Interviewed', *Act* (NZ), Vol. III, No. 2, Apr. 1982, p. 18-20. (On *The Opera of Guffaws*.)
Tom Vaughan, 'Artistic Marriage of Political Drama', *Morning Star*, 17 May 1982.

Michael Billington, 'Everybody's Favourite Fo', *The Guardian*, 26 Apr. 1983.

Tony Mitchell, 'Plotting to Create Mirth', *Glasgow Herald*, 3 May 1983. (On *Female Parts*.)

Steve Grant and Tony Mitchell, 'An Interview with Dario Fo and Franca Rame', *Theater*, Vol. XIV, No. 3, Summer/Fall, 1983, p. 43-9. (On *Female Parts*, *The Opera of Guffaws* and politics in Italy and the USA.)

Derek Boothman, 'Popular and Political Theatre', *Marxism Today*, Aug. 1983, p. 37-9. (On La Comune.)

Tony Mitchell, 'Open House with Dario Fo and Franca Rame', *Theater*, Vol. XV, No. 3, Summer/Fall, 1984, p. 65-8. (On *Open Couple*.)

Joseph Farrell, 'Women Need their Share of the Limelight', *The Scotsman*, 27 Sept. 1984. (On *Female Parts*.)

Scott Rosenberg, 'Dario Fo, Italy's Political Clown, Pays a Visit', *New York Times*, 25 May 1986.

Peter Rozovsky, 'Italian Pair are Finally Here', *The Guardian* (USA), 26 May, 1986.

Joseph Farrell, 'Fo and Rame', *Plays and Players*, June 1987, p. 9-10. (On *The Kidnapping of Francesca* and *The Actor's Manual*.)

b: Secondary Sources in English

Full-Length Studies

Tony Mitchell, *Dario Fo: People's Court Jester*, London: Methuen, 1984. Revised and expanded version, 1986.

David Hirst, *Dario Fo*, London: Macmillan, 1988.

Articles and Chapters in Books

A. Richard Sogliuzzo, 'Dario Fo: Puppets for a Proletarian Revolution', *The Drama Review*, Vol. XVI, No. 3, Sept. 1972, p. 72-7. (On Nuova Scena).

Suzanne Cowan, 'The Throwaway Theatre of Dario Fo', *The Drama review*, Vol. XIX, No. 2, June 1975, p. 103-13. (On Nuova Scena and the early years of La Comune.)

Suzanne Cowan, 'Theatre, Politics, and Social Change in Italy since the Second World War', *Theatre Quarterly*, Vol. VII, No. 27, Autumn 1977, p. 25-38. (The social, political and theatrical background to Fo's work.)

Tony Mitchell, 'Dario Fo's *Mistero Buffo*: Popular Theatre, the *Giullari*, and the Grotesque', *Theatre Quarterly*, Vol. IX, No. 35, Autumn 1979, p. 1-10.

Tony Mitchell, 'The Histrionics of Class Struggle', *Gambit*, Vol. IX,
No. 36, 1980, p. 55-60. (On *Ulrike Meinhof, Accidental Death,
Mistero Buffo,* and *Archangels Don't Play Pinball.*)

Charles Mann, 'Fo No-Show Doesn't Mean No Fo Show', *Village
Voice*, 17-23 Dec. 1980. (Overview, Fo's refused visa to the USA,
We Won't Pay! We Won't Pay!.)

Caroline Tisdall, 'The Collective Explosion', *The Guardian*,
1 Mar. 1980. (*Anarchist* in the West End.)

Sandy Craig, 'Accidental Staging of an Anarchist',
The Leveller, Apr. 1980, p. 26-7. (Interview with Gavin Richards
about the West End *Anarchist.*)

Mario B. Mignone, 'Dario Fo: Jester of the Italian Stage',
Italian Quarterly, No. 85, 1981, p. 47-62. (Overview to 1980.)

Lloyd Trott, 'So You Think that's Funny, Turning Rebellion into
Money', *The Leveller*, 21 Aug-3 Sept. 1981, p. 18-19. (On London
productions of *Anarchist, Can't Pay? Won't Pay!* and *Female Parts.*)

R. G. Davis, 'Dario Fo Off-Broadway: the Making of Left Culture under
Adverse Conditions', *Theatre Quarterly*, Vol. X, No. 40, Autumn-
Winter 1981, p. 30-6. (Davis' attempts to stage *We Won't Pay!* in the
USA).

David Groves, 'Laughter Has Become a Sghignazzo', *Act* (NZ),
Vol. VII, No. 2, Apr. 1982, p. 16-18. (On *The Opera of Guffaws.*)

Steve Grant, 'Laughter on the Ramparts', *Time Out*, 17-13 May 1982,
p. 6-11. (Biography, politics in Italy, *The Opera of Guffaws.*)

Vittorio Felaco, 'Notes on Text and Performance in the Theatre of Dario
Fo', in Michael Herzfeld and Margot D. Lenhart, eds.,
Semiotics 1980, New York: Plenum Press, 1982, p. 57-71. (Notes
towards a semiotic analysis of *Mistero Buffo.*)

Joel Schechter, 'Dario Fo's Obscene Fables', *Theater*, Vol. XIV, No. 1,
Winter 1982, p. 87-90.

Jim Hiley, 'Singing of Dark Times', *Observer Magazine*, 24 Apr. 1983,
p. 28-31. (Also in *Riverside Workshops* — overview, interview,
Obscene Fables.)

Brian Glanville, 'Master Class from a Master Clown', *Sunday Times*,
1 May 1983. (Also in *Riverside Workshops.*)

Vittorio Felaco, 'New Teeth for an Old Shark', in John Fuegi et al.,
eds., *Beyond Brecht: Brecht Yearbook Vol. 11*, 1982, Detroit:
Wayne State University Press, 1983, p. 57-71. (Fo and Rame as
inheritors of Brechtian theatre concepts; *The Opera of Guffaws.*)

Joel Schecter, 'Beyond Brecht: New Authors, New Spectators', in Fuegi,
op. cit., p. 43-53. (Fo as one of a number of modern playwrights who
have extended Brecht's precepts.)

Sally Banes, 'Dario Fo's Theater of Blasphemy', *Village Voice*,
2 Aug. 1983, p. 1, 33-5. (Overview and *Mistero Buffo.*)

Joel Schechter, 'The Un-American Satire of Dario Fo', *Partisan Review*, Vol. LI, No. 1, 1984, p. 112-19. (*Anarchist*, *We Won't Pay!* and *About Face* considered in the light of the USA visa refusal.)

Lino Pertile, 'Dario Fo', in Michael Ceasar and Peter Hainsworth, eds., *Writers and Society in Contemporary Italy*, New York: St. Martins, 1984, p. 167-190. (Overview to 1984.)

Joseph Farrell, 'Sending in the Clown to Fight Oppression', *The Scotsman*, 25 Aug. 1984. (On *Mistero Buffo*.)

Eric Bentley, 'Was This Death Accidental?', *Theater*, Vol. XVI, No. 2, Spring 1985, p. 66. (On the Broadway *Anarchist*.)

Martin W. Walsh, 'The Proletarian Carnival of Fo's *Non si paga!*', *Modern Drama*, Vol. XXVIII, No. 2, June 1985, p. 211-22.

Joel Schechter, 'Dario Fo: the Clown as Counter-Informer', in *Durov's Pig: Clowns, Politics and Theater*, New York: Theatre Communications Group, 1985, p. 142-57. (On *We Won't Pay!*, *Accidental Death*, *About Face* and *Throw the Lady Out*).

Serena Anderlini, 'Franca Rame: Her Life and Works', *Theater*, Vol. XVII, No. 1, Winter 1985, p. 32-9. (Detailed assessment of Rame's career from childhood to *Elizabeth*.)

Ron Jenkins, 'Dario Fo: the Roar of the Clown', *The Drama Review*, Spring 1986, p. 172-79. (On *Mistero Buffo* and *Tale of a Tiger*.)

Ron Jenkins, 'Clowns, Politics and Miracles: the Epic Satire of Dario Fo', *American Theater*, Vol. III, No. 3, June 1986. (Similar to the above.)

R. G. Davis, 'Seven Anarchists I Have Known: American Approaches to Dario Fo', *New Theatre Quarterly*, Vol. II, No. 8, Nov. 1986, p. 313-19.

Reference Sources

Suzanne Cowan, *The Militant Theatre of Dario Fo*, Ph.D. Thesis, University of Minnesota, 1977.

'Dario Fo', in Michael Anderson et al., eds., *A Handbook of Contemporary Drama*, London: Pitman, 1974, p. 152-3.

Suzanne Cowan, 'Dario Fo: Bibliography, Biography, Playography', *Theatre Checklist No. 17*, 1978.